European Foundation
for the Improvement of
Living and Working Conditions

✍ **W9-CIP-704**

Family Care of Dependent Older People in the European Community

EF/93/27/EN

Relatives "deposit at the hospital this old
draining body, asking us to keep it whole
to ward off their guilt so that they can find
again in their hearts and in their homes
the person who was their father or mother".

Catherine Delarue[1]

---

1   "Aïeul entre ascendents et descendants" in Revue Pratique de
Psychologie et de la Vie sociale et d'Hygiène mentale, No. 2/3,
1988 (pp 15-21), p 16.

European Foundation
for the Improvement of
Living and Working Conditions

Family Care of Dependent Older People in the European Community

Hannelore Jani-Le Bris
CLEIRPPA

Centre de Liaison, d'Étude, d'Information et de Recherche
sur les Problèmes des Personnes Âgées

Loughlinstown House,
Shankill, Co. Dublin, Ireland
Tel: +353 1 282 6888   Fax: +353 1 282 6456

Cataloguing data can be found at the end of this publication

Luxembourg: Office for Official Publications of the European Communities, 1993

ISBN 92-826-6355-8

Printed in Ireland

PREFACE

The implications of an ageing population for both living and working conditions have occupied an important place in the European Foundation's programmes of work over the last decade. In particular, an extensive analysis of the situation of older people in the European Community was published in 1987 as **Meeting the Needs of the Elderly**. This report showed that the population of people over pension age and especially those aged 80 and over, is rising in all EC countries; it drew attention to the needs for care and support for these older elderly. The current studies have specifically looked at the situation of those who provide most of the care to dependent older people - their families, especially spouses and daughters.

The Foundation's studies have sought to document systematically the needs and experiences of these family carers, and to assess the impact of caring on daily life. Research was undertaken in all Member States, with the exception of Luxembourg. These national studies look, in particular, at policy developments and initiatives to assist family carers, with a view to identifying what can be done to improve the quality of life for carers, as well as for their dependent older relatives. Of course the nature and extent of supportive services varies significantly between the Member States, even though they share a common emphasis upon maintaining older people at home, in the community, for as long as possible.

The main consolidated report of this study, published as this volume, does not replay all the data from the different national reports, but aims to present a general picture of the carers' situations, problems and sources of help. It draws upon statistical data, but also upon interviews with family carers. While differences are discussed - between male and female carers, those living with the older person and those living separately, and between countries - the report highlights much that is common to the experience of carers across the Member States.

The results, conclusions and recommendations of the report were presented to an evaluation committee of the Foundation's Administrative Board in September 1992. The group, composed of representatives of employers' organisations, trades unions and governments in the Member States welcomed the information and its presentation. Their debate underlined the importance of trends in ageing and needs for care, and the urgency for considering implications in both the workplace and the community. While social policies increasingly emphasise care in and by the family, other trends in the labour market, household structures, public finances and social values - make competing demands on family resources. In recognising family care as the cornerstone of care for older people, the groups identified concerns about the prospects for extending supportive services in the future.

In this European Year of Older People and Solidarity between the Generations the Foundation is pleased to contribute reports* which offer information, analyses and ideas intended to support discussions about improving welfare and quality of life for older people and their families.

Clive Purkiss
Director

* 1. Family care of the older elderly : Casebook of initiatives
M.A.G.A. Steenvorden, F.G.E.M. van der Pas, N.G.J. de Boer

2. Carers talking : Interviews with family carers of older dependent people in the European Community
Elizabeth Mestheneos, Judith Triantafillou (eds.)

3. Eldercare and employment : Workplace policies and initiatives to support workers who are carers
Marina Hoffmann, George Leeson

C O N T E N T S

LIST OF STATISTICAL TABLES AND GRAPHS

If male children do not want to nourish
their father or mother, nobody
forces them to; daughters are
obliged to do this,
even when they are not willing.

Herodotus[1]

---

1   Quoted in Minois, G., Histoire de la Vieillesse: de l'Antiquité à la Renaissance, Fayard, Paris, 1987.

INTRODUCTION

This report, as well as the 11 national reports on which it is essentially based, is part of the fourth four-year rolling programme of the European Foundation for the Improvement of Living and Working Conditions[1], which runs from 1989 to 1992 [European Foundation, 1989]. The end of the programme will, then, coincide with the opening of the *Single Market* and the launching of the EC's *Year of the Elderly and of Solidarity between the Generations* in 1993.

As one of its priority actions, the Foundation set up a research team in early 1989. The purpose of this team, including representatives of the 12 Member States, was to investigate the experiences of people caring for an elderly relative.

The research team and its work were directed by the Foundation's officer, Robert Anderson. Between Spring 1989 and Summer 1991, the team met six times[2]; representatives of international bodies[3] attended the main co-ordination meetings.

---

1   Loughlinstown House, Shankill, Co. Dublin, Ireland.

2   May 1989 in Ireland; November 1989 in France; July 1990 in Spain; December 1990 in the Netherlands; March 1991 in Greece; and June 1991 in Belgium.

3   Commission of the European Communities; Council of Europe; European Social Policy Research Centre; Economic and Social Committee; Confederation of Family Organisations in the European Community; European Trade Unions Confederation; European Research into Consumer Affairs; FIGED; OECD; UN.

From the outset, national descriptions of the situation of the elderly and of the family's role in caring for the older elderly highlighted two things: firstly, the deeply rooted and widely held belief that families are disengaging from their elderly relatives is in reality unfounded anywhere in Europe; and secondly, accurate data on the family care of the elderly are lacking in most Member States: it is only in the UK, Ireland and (to a lesser extent) Denmark that representative research has been conducted at national level, producing detailed information on the situation of carers. Two other Member States have started conducting research in this area: Germany (though only a preliminary report on the national survey [Schneekloth, 1992] is available at the time of writing) and France, where the section *Recherche de la Caisse Vieillesse* (Research Department of the Pensions Office) has recently launched a representative national survey.

In 1990 the Foundation initiated research on family carers in the EC's Member States. This report is a synthesis of the 11 national reports[1]. It is not in any way a substitute for a reading of the individual national reports, particularly since most of the details given in them will not be repeated here. For anybody interested in the national reports, a full list is included in Annex 2.

---

1   There is no report for Luxembourg; the data on the situation in Luxembourg used for this synthesis come from other sources. The report for Germany does not include the former German Democratic Republic.

Objectives

The fundamental aim of the research programme is to obtain and disseminate improved knowledge of family carers' in the European Community. It is intended to assess their needs and their ability to cope with the burden as well as the implications and consequences of caring for an elderly relative, usually an ageing parent or spouse.

Another key objective is to provide each Member State with a means of comparing its situation with those of other countries, and therefore to see how public policy can influence institutional change and service provision.

The objectives defined by the Foundation can be summarized as follows:

[]   to provide information on the extent and nature of family care for older people;

[]   to increase knowledge of the various factors likely to affect trends in family care;

[]   to examine the services and benefits provided for carers and, more generally, policies to support them;

and, in compliance with the Foundation's role,

[]   to draw up socio-political recommendations concerning carers.

Methodology

The adopted method of work was essentially *desk research:* work was restricted to the examination of existing data, owing both to the high cost of conducting representative national surveys of family carers. Field research was nonetheless conducted in six countries: Germany, France, Greece, the Netherlands, Portugal and Spain.

To ensure comparability, the 11 national reports adhered to an
identical work plan and to two basic definitions: *the family carer* is a
person who is related to the person he or she is caring for either by
blood or by **marriage**[1], and the person being cared for should **be over**
the **age of 74**. The concept of *dependence*, however, has not been tied to
any rigid common definition, since there are considerable disparities
both between one country and another and between one research study and
another. Dependence may thus be of either a physical or mental nature.
In practice analyses of demographic and other changes were generally
able to maintain the 'age' criterion but most of the research on caring
is defined by dependency and not by age. The initial decision to focus
research on people over the age of 74 was because advanced age is one
of the factors determining loss of autonomy and its corollary, the need
for care. This decision was respected in the samples studied by the six
pieces of field research (see above), but proved impossible to apply in
the desk research because this age threshold is not always used in the
reference material.

Both desk and field research were divided into five main areas:

1. **General context**: demographic aspects, particularly as regards the
    population aged 75 and over; services for the elderly; the
    dependence and health of people aged 75 or over; main trends
    affecting family structure.

2. **Carers**: who they are and what they do; the decision-making process
    to become a carer; changes in the caring situation and the factors
    that determine these changes; daily dimensions of caring; carers'
    situation and employment; the positive aspects of caring.

---

1   This is based on the definition of the family as 'a succession of
    individuals who are descended from each other, and those who are
    related to them by marriage' (Lalande, 1968); this includes
    collateral branches.

3. **Assistance and policies for carers:** practical, financial and psychological support; information and training; access to assistance; use and acceptance of formal and informal assistance; unsatisfied needs.

4. **The costs of caring:** social costs; psychological costs; financial costs; costs in terms of the carer's health.

5. **Carers' perspectives on their future:** limits and alternatives to caring; how caring will end; carers' plans for the future.

The conclusions of each national report looked at current key issues in caring, in the eyes of policy-makers and service providers.

Field research was based on twenty-four[1] semi-directive interviews in each of the six countries concerned; these interviews were held with main carers for a relative aged at least 75 and who was dependent or losing their autonomy[2].

Interviews were held with a selected non-representative, range of carers so that the broadest possible picture of the situation could be obtained; this meant that each sample had to include:

[] 12 urban and 12 rural (not necessarily agricultural) carers;

[] at least 4 men;

[] at least 6 caring spouses;

[] at least 4 (male or female) carers who were in paid employment, even if only during the early days of caring.

---

1   Twelve in the Netherlands.

2   Dependence could be physical and/or psychological. People who had been handicapped from birth or disabled as the result of an accident were excluded.

Since interviews would be affected both by national conditions and by the individual situation of the carer concerned, researchers were left to decide upon the structure of the interview. Their content concentrated on the issues included under headings 2-5 of the desk research, but they had to bring to light any specific details pertaining to the carer being interviewed (e.g. a combination of caring and occupational activity; disfunction of family life caused by dementia of the person being cared for; the fact that the carer was a man; the strong cohesion [or lack of it] of the family group; role reversal).

It was also intended that interviews and their analysis should place particular emphasis on the problems encountered by carers, on the burden, and on the help they needed to enable them to continue caring.

The results of this field research are contained in separate sections of the national reports but are integrated in the various sections and sub-sections of this European synthesis.

Case studies were the third aspect of the research work. Each national researcher was asked to present at least two case studies in which examples of good practice in caring for carers were examined and analysed in accordance with a defined procedure. The initiatives selected as case studies could relate to any area of assistance (financial, social, practical, material, psychological), and could be in the private or public sector, statutory or voluntary. Researchers were required to assess these initiatives critically, particularly as regards their success and transferability.

The case studies are not taken into consideration in this synthesis. They are the subject of another report, the *Case-Book*, being drawn up for the Foundation by the Dutch institute, NIZW.

A word of caution

The availability of reliable data varies enormously from one country to another. Discrepancies and gaps are evident as regards demographic statistics, since national censuses do not follow the same definitions

or the same schedules, either for implementation or for publication[1].
Gaps exist in national statistics concerning services for the elderly,
be they domiciliary or institutional: little information is available
on the number of different services, their scope, the number of users
or users' main characteristics (age, sex, marital status). Not all
Member States even know the proportion of people aged 75 or over who
are in institutions.

Systematic information on old people being cared for by their families,
on the number and characteristics of carers, the tasks they perform and
the volume of care they provide is scarce or non-existent.

Like the national reports, this synthesis is, therefore, based on
incomplete information; it aims to identify some of the key data that
would be useful to strengthen public policies for older people and
their family carers.

A second point that needs to be emphasized is the fact that most
research on family care tends to focus on carers of people who are
heavily dependent and therefore in need of **considerable help.** But
family care comes in *all shapes and guises*, ranging from (and sometimes
being limited to) occasional, small acts, to full-time caring, with all
the restrictions that implies for the carer.

Finally, we should like to point out that in this report we shall
mention only the bibliographical sources that are additional to those
cited in the national reports; those already mentioned in such reports
will be referred to only if they constitute an essential source
document for this synthesis.

---

1   For example, the breakdown by composition of the household may be
    done by individual or by household. Breakdowns by age, sex and
    marital status are rarely available, for the same period for all 12
    Member States, the exception being 1981/82 [Eurostat, 1989].
    Another example: sheltered housing may be categorised as private
    homes or institutions, depending on the definitions used by the
    census.

GENERAL CONTEXT

1. Overview

There are numerous factors that weave the backcloth on which European families' form attitudes and behaviours when a relative becomes dependent. They constitute the context in which adult children and spouses, often elderly themselves, take action when the parent or spouse reaches a stage at which he or she can no longer look after him or herself.

[] Changes in the traditional family structure.

[] The ageing of the population and, since relatively recently, the increase in the number and percentage of people who are very old and, as a result, more likely to be physically and/or psychologically dependent.

[] The uncertainty of even medium-term forecasts, from which demographics alone seems to escape because it is a field in which numerous factors of change remain constant; uncertainty here is caused rather by the fact that so many parameters remain unknown[1].

[] The total or partial failure, both quantitatively and qualitatively, of support structures for the elderly to meet needs; this applies to both domiciliary services and long or short-stay institutional services.

[] Negative perceptions of residential institutions which are deeply rooted and persist even though they are no longer always based on fact.

---

1 Changes in the economy, the labour market and the division of working/leisure time; developments in medical, pharmacological and biological research, as well as in family structures, social mores and ways of living, etc.

[] Cuts in public expenditure.

Throughout Europe, the family is the foundation of care for the elderly, almost irrespective of a country's family, social and socio-political structures. The omnipresence of the family in this sphere is largely unrecognised or unacknowledged by the general public even if they themselves are carers. They are misled by the common fallacy of family disengagement from its older members; this fallacy persists despite the fact that socio-political decision-makers in several Member States have begun to see the reality behind the myth. Perhaps it persists because this recognition of the facts has not been reflected in practical measures to support families in their caring role.

The virtual absence of effective help for family carers, the difficulties that people encounter to obtain help, the difficulty even in imagining that help might be available, in finding out what help they are entitled to, and in accepting it without feeling guilty - all this is at the centre of the problem facing carers. The caring resource is in many places on the brink of exhaustion, yet there is an immediate need to optimise (in terms of both quantity and quality) this caring structure, and place families and the elderly in a position in which they have real choice when they are faced with a situation of dependence, be it physical, psychological or social.

Social policies to support dependent older people are at very different stages of evolution in the 12 Member States. They are nevertheless everywhere based (in fact or in design) on the same two pillars: residential institutions (which may or may not provide nursing care) and, domiciliary services (in order to meet older people's expressed wish never to enter an institution, and more specifically to try to contain the high financial costs that are associated with residential care).

In other words, virtually all social policies actually count on, or entirely depend on the family - yet few Member States have taken any practical steps to provide that primary pillar with any real support. On the contrary, several Member States still have laws that hold the family responsible for its older members[1]. This means that there is an urgent need for practices and policies to improve family carers' living and working conditions - because caring for an old person is work.

2. Demographic context

Population changes

With its 327 million inhabitants, the Europe of Twelve yet has the third highest population in the world, preceded only by China (1104 million) and India (815 million) [Eurostat, 1991[2]]. But, since dear old Europe is really getting old, with a marked drop in population growth, it now accounts, despite its third position, for only 6% of the world's total population, as opposed to the 10% it represented in 1950 [D-1].

Natural population growth[3] was still positive in 1989, although there had been negative growth rates in two Member States, Germany and Denmark[4] [A-2]. Natural population increase[5] was high in 1989, with

---

1   For example, Germany and France have laws that make the family responsible for older members' basic needs, and Greece has a provision to this effect in its Constitution. Denmark, on the other hand, has laws that explicitly absolve the younger generations of responsibility for their forebears.

2   Most of the statistics used here have been drawn from this text. Hereafter, we shall simply indicate the number of the relevant table, e.g. [D-1].

3   i.e. the amount by which births exceed deaths.

4   Germany: -2.4 in 1975 and -0.3 in 1989. Denmark: -0.9 in 1985, 0.0 in 1988 and +0.4 in 1989.

5   Which also takes account of net migration.

a figure of +1.6 million [A-5], as opposed to +1.2 million in 1988 [Eurostat, 1990]. This 38% increase was mainly due to net migration into the Community (that) was higher than ever before "and that" results from the upheavals in Eastern Europe in 1989." [Eurostat, 1991]

Population ageing

In connection with demographic phenomena that have long-term repercussions, the increase in the proportion of old people in the total population is ineluctable: the primary, and for a long time the sole, cause is the drop in the birth-rate; the second more recent cause is the fall in the mortality rate. When referring to the age pyramid (see Figure 1)[1], there is evidence of the ageing of both the tip and the base which is the result of concomitant drops in fertility and mortality.

People aged under 15 represent no more than 18% of the Community's population (*young* populations have a very high proportion of people in this age bracket: e.g. 45% in Africa, only 3% of whose total population are aged 65 or over) [D-2].

At 1 January 1989[2], the **Community** had 46.6 million people aged **65 or over** (**14.3%** of the total population), 20.9 million (6.4%) of whom were aged 75 or over (see Table 1 and Figure 2).

National averages deviate little from these proportions, with the exception of Ireland, which is traditionally the *youngest* country in the Community[3].

---

1   Figures and tables are contained in Annex 3.

2   We refer to 1989 because we have breakdowns by age for all the Member States for that year, whereas the figures for Greece are missing in the statistics for 1 January 1990.

3   More precisely, 37% of the Irish are under the age of 20. This compares with 21% of Germans, and a Community average of 26% [B10].

Extremes values:

> 65 years: 11.1% Ireland - 15.6% UK

> 75 years: 4.4% Ireland - 7.4% Germany

It may, then, be stated that population ageing is a general trend in all the Member States and that the process is far from complete; according to Alain Parant, "the worst is still to come" [Parant, 1990], or, in Michel Loriaux's more optimistic words, "ageing will go from strength to strength" [Loriaux, 1989]. The history, the start of the ageing process, and its pace differ from one Member State to another.

The relative closeness of national rates of ageing in the years around 1990 masks major regional disparities in most countries. Most of these, however, can be attributed to internal migration: in brief, young people leave the countryside to set themselves up in industrialized areas, or areas that are being industrialized; they marry, have children and contribute to heavy urbanization of the area. Meanwhile, older people stay in their villages, whose loss of younger population is especially important in rural areas, distant from the zones of development. This contrast is most evident between north and south in Italy, and between coastal and inland regions in countries such as Spain, Portugal, Greece and Ireland.

Life expectancy

Life expectancy **at birth** has been rising continuously since the beginning of the century, when for example in France, it was, with very little exaggeration, about the same as it is now for a person who has taken early retirement - namely about forty years.

In 1960 in the European Community, life expectancy at birth for **men** was 67.3 years; just three decades later (1989) it had risen to **72.8**; the equivalent figures for **women** were **72.7** and **79.2** years. Women outlived men by an average of 5.4 years in 1960 and by 6.4 years in 1989. This inequality before death is least marked in Greece (5.0 years) and most marked in France (8.2 years). Also topping the list, French women can expect to live for 80.7 years[1] (1989), followed closely by Dutch

---

1   All figures relate to 1989, unless otherwise stated.

women, who have a life expectancy at birth of 79.9 years. For men, statistics promise the longest lives to the Dutch (73.7 years) followed by the Spaniards and Italians (73.2 years in 1987 and 1988 respectively).

The Europeans who have drawn the *short straw* as regards life expectancy at birth are Irish women (77.0 years) and men in Luxembourg (70.6 years, but in 1985/87), Portugal (70.9 years) and Ireland, again (71.0 years) (see Table 2).

Life expectancy at the **age of 75** is also rising, though the difference between men and women begins to diminish at this age; ranging from 1.0 year in Greece to 3.0 years in the Netherlands (the Community average is unknown).

Of those who survive to the age of 75, people living in Spain, France and the Netherlands have the longest life expectancy, whilst those living in Greece, Luxembourg and Ireland can expect to live the fewest years.

Life expectancy at the age of 75 - extreme values:

Women: [] 11.9 years in France; 11.4 years in the Netherlands;
       11.1 years in Spain (1987) and Denmark;
       [] 9.0 years in Ireland and 9.4 years in Greece.

Men: [] 9.2 years in Spain (1987) and France;
       [] 7.0 years in Ireland and 7.5 years in Luxembourg
          (1985/87).
       (see Table 2)

Predominance of women

In the EC, some 1055 boys are born for every 1000 girls. Because of men's higher mortality, their predominance diminishes over the years: the numbers are about equal between the ages of 45 and 50, then the balance swings in the other direction, and women become the more numerous. The proportion of women in the EC is 59% in the 60+ age bracket, and 69% in the 80+ bracket.

Just as men's and women's life expectancies and the difference between them vary from one Member State to another, so the percentages of women as a function of age also vary (see Table and figure 3). The preponderance of women is at its least pronounced in Greece (60% in the 80+ age bracket) and, conversely, is most pronounced in Germany (72%), Luxembourg (71%), Belgium and the UK (70%).

In all Member States, the proportion of women rises with age.

Extreme values – 65-69 years and $\geq$ 95 years, respectively:

[] Slight increase	Greece:	54% – 66%
[] Marked increase	France:	55% – 83%
	UK:	54% – 84%
	Luxembourg:	60% – 100%

The preponderance of women is, then, quite obviously one of the main demographic features of elderly populations, a general rule that Greece alone manages to evade (though at the price of the lowest life expectancy in Europe).

Marital status

Sex and age both have a role to play in the distribution of marital status. Widowhood is the major social risk faced by women, and it is a particular threat for women who have not been in paid employment which would entitle them to a retirement pension in their own right[1].

---

1   Under most of the retirement systems currently in force in Europe, the amount of old-age pensions is dependent on how long a person has paid social-security contributions. These systems also tend to provide for payment of a widow's pension, representing a proportion of the old-age pension her deceased husband would have received.

Widowhood is first and foremost a woman's problem: the European Community has (1981-82)[1] [EUROSTAT, 1988[2]] 16.6 million widows and widowers over the age of 64,[3] of whom only 18% are men. The 9 million widows and widowers aged 75 or over divide in precisely the same proportions: 81% of them are women.

The inequality of the sexes before death in the EC is such that, in the 75+ age bracket, there are as many widows among women (67%) as there are married among men (63%).

The risk of social isolation, usually as a result of the absence of a spouse, is reinforced among women also because they have a greater proclivity than men towards remaining single (12% of women but only 6% of men in the 75+ age group never married).

Altogether, the likelihood of moving into old age as one of a couple and of being able to count on mutual, complementary support within a partnership, is slight for women and strong for men. Over the age of 84, when people typically become less able to care for themselves, 41% of men and only 7% of women are still married. Since the man is also often older than his wife, he may enjoy well into his late age a *multi-faceted, personal and personalized service within his home* - his wife acting as the housewife, carer, night-and-day nurse, cook, charwoman and companion; and sometimes he might also be lucky enough to enjoy the further benefits of affection, understanding and tenderness. Even if

---

1   This is the most recent period for which the Statistical Office of the European Communities has a breakdown for all the Member States by the three variables of sex, age and marital status. Several of the national reports on carers give more recent figures, but these do not always refer to the same year. The national reports have, however, revealed that there has been very little change since 1981/82.

2   Table 3, recalculated.

3   Seventy three per cent of all widows and widowers are 65 or over.

for purely demographic reasons, few elderly women enjoy such good fortune in facing the adversity inherent in increasing dependence. National deviations from the European averages are slight, with only a few exceptions (see Table 4). Firstly, there is the case of Ireland, which traditionally tends to stand aside from the other Member States in terms of demographics: here there is both a high birth-rate and a high level of remaining single – 25% of those aged 75 or over are unmarried, with concomitantly smaller proportions of married people, widows and widowers.

At the other extreme, both geographically and demographically, Greece has the EC's lowest proportions of elderly never-married (4% of those aged 75 or over) and of widowers (22%), and thus, necessarily, has the highest proportions of married men (73% as against 47% in Ireland) and women (28% as against 15% in Ireland).

Finally, Greece, Italy and Ireland are characterized by the total or virtual absence of divorced people in the 75+ age bracket.

For a more detailed analysis of these phenomena, the reader is referred to Table 5, which gives a breakdown by sex, marital status, and by five-year age brackets.

Summary

The inequality of the sexes before death, and also before dependence, has considerable socio-demographic repercussions, which are essentially reflected in:

[]   the numerical predominance of women;

[]   the prevalence of widows;

[]   the higher rate of disability among the most numerous group, i.e. women.

These three phenomena become more pronounced as age increases.

3. Changes in family structure

Major trends

This vast subject, which is primarily the domain of family historians and sociologists, was tackled in the national reports essentially from the point of view of demographic indicators.

Since the beginning of this century, European societies have witnessed significant changes in family structures that are rooted in the history of each individual country. These changes have arisen as a result of the impact firstly of industrialization and then of post-industrial events. Broadly speaking, Member States have either abandoned or are in the process of abandoning the model of the traditional family. Danish society seems to have moved furthest along this path of change, whereas the Mediterranean countries, Portugal and Ireland are still largely in the grip of the model of the traditional family.

Faithful to a traditional pattern of behaviour in the face of change, human beings, confronted with changes in family structure, tend to idealize the past and refuse to acknowledge the value of the new. "The air of France still bears a hint of the intoxicating belief in the great rural family, in which relationships were idyllic and the generations intermingled without difficulty, to the great good of all." [Brisepierre, 1987] As the author urges, "family historians are there to correct idealized views of the past."[1]

The decline of the traditional family structure is often confused with a loss of all its values. In fact, it does not seem that, at any stage of the transition from the traditional to the more *modern* model, either affective family bonds or family solidarity are diminished – rather, they remain intact in a changed and changing framework.

---

1   Life expectancy in those times meant that three generations rarely co-existed and, if they did, it was only for a brief period. Even at the beginning of the twentieth century, a large number of children were orphaned, lost a sister or a brother and never knew any of their four grandparents.

This is reflected in, for example, a fact confirmed by virtually all the national reports: the omnipresence of the family in the care of dependent, elderly relatives.

Features of the modern family model

One of the primary features of the modern model of the family is that the generations tend **not to live together.**

In Denmark, where the transition appears to be at its most advanced, and for which there are detailed statistics, children do not stay in the parental home (which about half of them leave between the ages of 16 and 24) and return to it only in very rare cases. More particularly, the co-residence of adults and their elderly relatives has become a rare phenomenon (affecting at most 5% of those aged 80 or over). It is significant that only 1% of Danes aged between 40 and 64 say that they would like to live later with one of their children rather than continue living alone, should they find themselves in a difficult situation. The dominant model, for all age groups, is the single-person household[1] and the cohabiting couple (married or no), who may or may not have children. The *modern* Danish family is, then, based on the nuclear model.

As to whether relationships within the family network have changed, only 7% of elderly Danes have neither children, grandchildren nor siblings, and this 7% comprises mainly women aged 80 or over. People aged 70-95 who live in their own homes have frequent contact with their children (72% see them at least once a month and 44% see them at least three times a month), grandchildren (68% and 41% respectively) and brothers and/or sisters (43% and 17%) [Holstein, 1991].

Denmark is the EC's most highly developed Welfare State, its government's social policy does not see the family as a potential source of care for the elderly: the State defines for itself

---

1 Single-person households currently account for 15% of the total population, 43% of those aged 60 or over, 53% of those aged 70 or over and 66% or those aged 80 or over.

responsibility as the main carer. Nevertheless as the report for Denmark emphasises, in practice families and particularly spouses provide basic care and support.

Features of the traditional model

One of the main features of this model is the co-residence of various members of the family group, often including several families, generations or branches.

The **Spanish** report underlines that, particularly in rural areas, the family is responsible for caring for the elderly, who perform certain functions in exchange. The older generations have a central social role within the extended family and often have a degree of power deriving from their status as owners of the land. Also, the fact that they remain active and contribute to the material life of the family group guarantees their integration in the social network, particularly in the agricultural areas.

The **Italian** report points to the emergence of a trend against co-residence in the highly industrialized north of the country, but stresses the continuing influence of the extended family, particularly in the south. This model is characterized by relations of mutual support and solidarity, including, among others, the care of older relatives. Despite considerable change, the predominant social pattern is the refusal to abandon elderly relatives, a pattern that is reinforced by the relative lack of services for the elderly.

The **Greek** report stresses the importance of the family in the country's social structure, which is reinforced by the fact that people in urban areas tend to marry late and that, for both psychological and financial reasons, children tend to be slow to leave the parental home. Although Greek society is beginning to undergo radical changes (industrialization, urbanization) that are not without impact on the family structure, [Ziomas, 1991], the traditional family is holding very firm and its responsibility, particularly for its elderly, is rooted in the Constitution.

Another fundamental feature distinguishes the two models: **the _modern_ family tends to exclude death,** as is indicated by the fact that it is less common for people to die in their own homes, whereas the traditional family confronts death as a collective experience.

Summary

Fundamental changes are affecting family life, personal lives, ageing and old age. Social indicators bear witness to these changes and define the features of modern societies. The major trends in the EC are a drop in the marriage and birth-rates, accompanied by later marriages and births; an increase in divorce and remarriage, which disturbs the clarity of family trees; an increase in cohabitation and births outside marriage, as well as single parenthood; restructuring of the composition of households because of the move away from co-residence and the increase in single-person households; changes in marital relations, with the traditional marriage being transformed into a partnership of two financially independent and, therefore, more equal individuals; and finally, labour-market indicators, such as the increase in occupational activity among women and reduced working times (shorter working week, more paid leave, early retirement).

4. Assessment of dependence

A word of caution

In consideration of the gaps in basic data, the research reports give only limited descriptions of dependency; few representative national surveys have been conducted in the Member States. The works cited in the national reports are, therefore, disparate: they relate to different reference years; they rarely relate to a period of any length; they are often only regional; they may concern different age groups; one work points to the subjective perception of health, others concentrate on the degrees of difficulty encountered in performing the most common Activities of Daily Living (ADL), but measure those degrees of difficulty differently.

Overall, the national reports give the clear impression that the Member States have only incomplete knowledge of the health, degrees of incapacity and consequent needs of their elderly populations.

It is, therefore, impossible to make any reliable comparison between the Member States; the most we can do is to provide some indicators and identify general trends.

Thresholds of risk of dependency

Even though the majority of Europeans remain relatively, if not totally, **able-bodied to a good age,** a large number of them are affected by some incapacitating illness or disability and many of them have serious health problems, suffer from fatigue or feebleness as a result of old age. More frail than they were in their younger years, the elderly are more vulnerable to accidents and, being weaker, recover from them with more difficulty and more slowly. And it is also true (doubtless for countries other than Germany, though this is the country the following statement refers to) that "despite their sufferings, old people do not necessarily feel they need help or care; quite the contrary, their statements on this issue belie the supposed tendency to complain." [Infratest, 1991b]

All the national reports point to the acknowledged association between advancing age and physical and mental deterioration. Several authors stress that there are various risk thresholds for dependence, whose existence is revealed by any analysis, by age group, of people's assessment of their health or the difficulties they have in performing the Activities of Daily Living (ADL) (see Tables 6 and 7).

In as far as one can generalize about the very varied situations at both national and regional level within the Community, it would seem that a first risk threshold lies at about the age of 75 and that people enter a period of high risk as they approach 85, at least in the Member States of northern Europe, where social protection has long been provided. In Spain and Italy, the first risk threshold appears to be reached at the age of 70-74, with the second high-risk period beginning around the age of 80 in Italy and somewhat later in Spain. Clearly, in addition to differences between countries, the age at which people are at high risk for disability varies with gender and social class.

It is obvious that the risk thresholds identified are of **indicative value**; the *ADL scales* show that thresholds vary from one type of activity to another (see below).

Research work conducted in some countries also points to a general improvement in the health of elderly populations over the past few years, at least in the countries of northern Europe. According to a series of Belgian surveys (1967 - 1976 - 1985), the proportion of elderly people who were able-bodied rose from 75% to 82% over these periods [Nijkamp et al, 1991, p 93] (although the bibliographical source used fails to define the concept of elderly and a high non-response rate of 30% discredits the 1985 findings). According to two consecutive surveys conducted in Northern Italy (1980-83), the percentage of people over the age of 64 who claimed to be in good health rose from 61% to 67%; the questionnaire did, however, limit the response options simply to "good" or "poor" [Espace Social Européen, 1991, p 128]. For the Netherlands, two comparable sets of data exist: in 1955-57, 33% of those aged 75 or over (living in their own homes or in institutions) had difficulty in climbing stairs; in 1982, the situation seemed to have improved for those living in their own homes:

Netherlands, 1982	Men	Women
Living in own home > 75 years	22%	28%
In an institution > 80 years	60%	81%

[ibid]

The health of old people in Ireland was also noted to have improved [O'Shea, 1991].

And finally, French research indicates that the threshold for high-risk of dependency was around the age of 75 in the 1970s and is closer to the age of 85 nowadays.

The most common disabling illnesses

All the national reports that mention illnesses agree on the predominance of those affecting the skeletal-muscular system (particularly arthrosis and arthritis), the respiratory system and the cardio-vascular system[1]. The reports are unanimous in pointing to the susceptibility to **multiple illnesses** in old age.

Several of the national reports stress the **chronic** nature of these illnesses, whose number, seriousness and **debilitating effects** increase considerably with age. This also explains the heavy concentration of both health expenditure and need for care on the very old elderly.

The German analysis lays particular emphasis on the fact that increased life expectancy at advanced ages, and the progress made in medical research have together led to a considerable increase in the elderly population's need for health care. This paradox derives from the fact that antibiotics and vaccines, for example, reduce the mortality rates but increase the risk of chronic illnesses against which medicine is largely ineffective and from which people were *saved* until recently by early death.

Mental deterioration

Senile dementia, in its different guises, really deserves a long chapter to itself because of the particularly onerous problems and concerns raised by the care of people suffering from it, both at the socio-political level and at the level of the day-to-day burden assumed by families.

Problems in making specific diagnoses are one reason that very few reliable data are available. As an indication, all the figures provided by the national reports are combined in a single table though they are not truly comparable (different reference years, different definitions and different age groups) (see Table 8).

---

1   The data available are nonetheless too insubstantial to be used to draw up a table of the most prevalent diseases.

It appears that the number of old people affected by mental deterioration is increasing because of the drop in mortality among the older elderly: in years gone by, death would have intervened before illnesses of this kind became apparent. In addition to this, there are no pharmacological treatments for the various forms of senility and progress in research in this field is slow. The Danish report concludes that "the risk of senility increases exponentially with age and, as the number of elderly increases, an increase of 50 000-70 000 in the number with senile dementia is expected within the next 20 years, **if no new treatments are discovered**." Dependence as a result of mental deterioration is often accompanied by incontinence, agitation (being unable to stay still) and failure to communicate or cooperate [O'Shea, 1991, p 14], with loss of memory being at the core of the problem.

The authors of the German report point to the fact that there is less chance of old people being cared for "informally", i.e. by their families, once they are suffering from mental disorders.

Mobility

Many old people have problems with their locomotor system; generally speaking, the size of their *geographical field* of mobility diminishes with age, the extreme being confinement, firstly to the home and then to bed (though this last stage is reached in only rare cases). There is a need to distinguish between more or less *voluntary* confinement - when people have no need or desire to go out, have lost their enthusiasm, are lazy, or simply reduce their activities outside the home and their immediate social network - and confinement caused by physical limitations.

The proportion of old people who are **bed-ridden** is small, though it varies with age and from country to country:

B	1985	?	1%	[Nijkamp, 1991 b: 93]
D[1]	1991	$\geq$ 70 years	3%	Population living in their own home [Infratest, 1991: 43]

---

1 Including the former GDR.

DK	1988	$\geq$ 70 years	1%	Population living in their own home
		$\geq$ 80 years	1%	" "
F	1982	75-84 years	2%	
		$\geq$ 85 years	5%	77% of whom were living in their own home
P	1987	75-84 years	3%	
		$\geq$ 85 years	7%	

The proportion may be higher among women: 1% of German men and 5% of German women in the same age group. The opposite applies in Portugal, where 8% of men and 7% of women aged 85 or over are bed-ridden.

Only the Portuguese report indicates the proportion of people who are **wheelchair-bound**: 0.6% of those aged 75-84 and 1.8% of those aged 85 and over. A recent survey in France of those in receipt of retirement pensions for management staff (aged 80 or over) indicates that 2% of them use a wheelchair [Jani-Le Bris and Luquet, 1992]. Another French survey, this time of a more underprivileged population group (people in rural areas who are aged 60 or over and have a home-help), gives a figure for the proportion of wheelchair users that is twice as high as this [Jani-Le Bris, 1990].

Similarly, few figures are available on **confinement to the home:**

DK	1988	Population living in their own home, as %
			men	women	total
		70-79 years	5	10	8
		$\geq$ 80 years	17	32	27
F	1982	Population living in their own home
		75-84 years			11
		$\geq$ 85 years			29

Clearly **mobility** does not depend only on the **locomotor system**, but also, and sometimes solely, on **sharpness of vision, physical co-**

ordination, agility or obesity. The Danish authors point out that "the fact that people's **toenails** are badly cut may help to reduce mobility". The proportions of older people who are incapable of looking after their own feet are high: 52% of those aged 80 or over in Denmark, 65% of those aged 85 or over in Italy and 27% of those aged 65 or over in the UK (see Table 6).

To complete the information on the causes of reduced mobility, account must be taken of data on vision:

DK   23% of people aged 70 or over have problems with their sight (1986/87).

E   3% of elderly people (age not defined) are blind and 30% (24% of men and 37% of women) suffer from poor vision (1987).

GR   Of the users of local centres for the elderly (KAPI), who are a specific population group in that their attendance at these centres implies a certain degree of mobility, 26% of men and 15% of women over the age of 74 are blind (1985).

I   31% of people aged 75 or over "are affected by blindness" [Espace Social Européen, 1991, p 128]. (Presumably this does not refer only to those who are totally blind.)

IRE   16% of men and 22% of women aged between 70 and 79 have difficulty in reading a newspaper; the percentages rise to 36% of men and 44% of women aged 80 or over (1982) [ibid, p 119].

NL   9% of people aged 75 or over are either blind or suffering from severe visual impairment (1990).

Difficulties in daily living

In social research on the elderly, a certain consensus has been reached through the work conducted over the past ten years or so using ADL (*Activities of Daily Living*) scales. These scales are a measuring instrument that is standardised and easy to use. Respondents are asked identical questions on a series of daily activities, the answers to which indicate their level of independence. The questions and response options are simple[1].

The available results of ADL studies from several Member States indicate a certain standardization as regards the questions, but the response options are rather more variable (See Tables 6a and 6b). In broad terms, three categories of activity are distinguished, each being covered by a separate scale: self care[2], domestic activities[3] and "mobility"[4]. The most thorough surveys include a question on the use of an aid every time a response suggests that the respondent has difficulty in doing something; this means that the results also include information on the use of aids to perform Activities of Daily Living. Finally, the data collected are generally used to draw up categories of independence/dependence on the basis of the number of Activities of Daily Living respondents cannot perform.

---

1   Example: "Can you take a bath on your own?"
         *   Yes, easily
         *   Yes, but with some difficulty
         *   Yes, but with considerable difficulty
         *   No, only with help
         *   No, I cannot take a bath at all
     These five responses are often grouped under three or four headings.
     The bed-ridden are usually separated from the other groups.

2   Feeding oneself, dressing, cutting one's toenails, continence, etc.

3   Cooking, washing up, doing the day-to-day household chores, doing heavier housework, etc.

4   Getting up and going to bed, going to the toilet, moving around the house, going out, doing the shopping, etc.

In summarising the various findings available, the following major trends[1] can be identified, though of course, the definitions and groupings used are not the same in every survey.

[] In Member States in central and northern Europe (Germany, Belgium, France, Ireland and the UK), the majority (ranging from over 50% to over 60%) of people aged 75 or over are more or less without disability, and they can be deemed to be independent. For those aged 80 or over, this proportion falls below the 50% threshold, being lowest in France[2] at 38% (see Table 9).

[] The performance of basic actions (getting up or going to bed, feeding and washing oneself) is, in general, impossible for only a small minority (apparently less than 10%), even among the very old elderly.

Judging from the information available, this may not be true of the countries of southern Europe, at least not for Italy, where 17% of those over the age of 84 have difficulty in putting themselves to bed, or Portugal, where 18% say they have difficulty in feeding themselves without help.

By contrast, another basic action - dressing oneself - is a problem for more people, particularly once they reach their eighties: 40% of Irish women as against 19% of Danish men or women (plus 4% who actually need help), 37% of Portuguese and 21% of Italians (men and women over the age of 84) (see Tables 6a and 6b).

[] Taking a shower or bath are difficult activities, especially for the older elderly, though there are major variations from one country to another: 14% of Germans (aged 70 or over), 60% of Italians, 55% of Irish men and 72% of Irish women say that it is difficult or impossible for them to take a shower or bath without help. However, German homes are probably more likely to have a

---

1   Tables 6a and 6b do not give all the details contained in the national reports or drawn from other bibliographical sources.

2   This may be a result of differences in definition.

shower installed than are homes in Italy and Ireland, which means that, in their responses, the Italians and Irish would tend to be referring to bathing rather than showering - and a bath is far more difficult to cope with when one is no longer fully able-bodied (see Table 6).

[] Difficulty in moving around **indoors** is a problem for only a small minority in Germany, Belgium and the UK, but the percentages of old people in Denmark and Italy who experience this difficulty are, comparatively, high (see Table 6b).

[] Having difficulty in **moving about outside the home** is probably far more common, though there are almost no comparable figures on this.

It may be noted, however, that those who cannot move about outside alone account for 7% of those aged 65 or over in the UK, 13% of those aged 75 or over in Belgium and 20% of those aged 80 or over in Denmark.

Incontinence

There appear to be few data on this subject in the Member States. The information available refers to just three, very different, countries. Problems of incontinence (urinary and/or faecal) are suffered by 7% of Germans aged 70 or over[1], between 6% and 13% (depending on age) of Italians aged 75 or over[2] and of Greeks aged 65 and over living in

---

1   Ability to retain urine and faeces:
        *   89% without difficulty
        *   7% with difficulty
        *   1% impossible
        *   3% no response
  [Infratest, 1991]

2   Inability to control anal and urethral sphincters (regional surveys in northern Italy):
        *   75-79 years 6%
        *   80-84 years 13%
        * $\geq$ 85 years 13%

rural areas, 24% reported problems of urinary incontinence, and 13% of faecal incontinence [1].

Although the data are insufficient, it is likely that the proportion of incontinence-sufferers increases everywhere with age and that this type of problem is often combined with other pathologies and disabilities. It thus seems more than probable that many carers, be they spouses or children, are faced every day with a situation that is not only very distressing but also the cause of a great deal of additional work (keeping the old person clean, frequently changing and washing bed linen - not to mention the havoc that can be caused by the *scatological games* played by some seriously demented old people).

Higher rate of disability among women

The higher rate of disability among women has been confirmed in France by the survey on *Disability-free Life Expectancy* (see Table 10), in the UK by the national survey conducted in 1988 (Disability Survey), and in Germany by a similar national survey conducted in 1991[2] [Infratest, 1991].

But although, overall, a higher rate of disability among women may appear to be a general rule throughout Europe, several research works seem to suggest that the rule is not without its nuances:

[] The higher rate of disability among women derives essentially from problems affecting the **locomotor system**, since, as Dutch research

---

1   Of whom
    *   17.6% suffer occasional and 6.6% frequent urinary incontinence
    *   8.7% suffer occasional and 4.1% frequent faecal incontinence

2   At the time of writing (April 1992), only the preliminary report is available.

work points out [Kastelein, 1989, p 5), women are more likely than men to suffer from rheumatism, one of the predominant illnesses of old age. Wherever data are available, irrespective of the country concerned, it emerges that **old men are more able to walk about than old women**.

Here too, however, variations may emerge, depending on breakdown by age and sex. Thus, **Portuguese** figures suggest that, at ages of 85 and over, the gap between men and women narrows as regards their ability to climb stairs, though it remains very wide as regards the ability to walk. **Irish** figures point to the fact that the greater reduction in women's spatial autonomy begins and increases rapidly from the age of 75. **Danish** figures indicate a similar situation as regards difficulty in going out, beginning at the age of 80; in the case of being house-bound, however, the rate among women is double that among men, as from the age of 70 (see Table 11).

The general rule that women suffer a greater reduction in mobility than do men is, then, subject to variations from one country to another. The Portuguese figures suggest the following hypothesis: in Member States in southern Europe, men suffer as much as women from a loss of spatial autonomy. This hypothesis is supported by Greek data[1], but has yet to be verified.

[] The rule that the rate of disability is higher among women than men may well be invalidated in other areas, but there are far too few data to be able to confirm this hypothesis. The aforementioned **Dutch** research indicates that men suffer more than women from cardio-vascular diseases [Kastelein, 1989, p 5]. In **Belgium**, there is little difference between the percentages of men and women aged 80 or over who are disabled and who can not be left alone.

---

1   The higher rate of disability among women in the rural environment, which is incontestable between the ages of 65 and 84, disappears once people reach the age of 85.

In Germany, reduction in the ability to be self-sufficient[1] barely differs with gender. In **Denmark**, confinement to bed or a wheelchair affects equal proportions of old men and women. And in **Portugal**, the proportion of people who are bed-ridden is identical for men and women (3%) between the ages of 75 and 84; but above this age, the proportion of men (8%) who are bed-ridden is greater than the proportion of women (6%).

Health and entry into an institution

Old people living in institutions are more disabled than are their counterparts living in their own homes - but they are also older. This does not in any way alter the fact that the very large majority of dependent old people live in their own homes: as many as eight out of ten.

Several of the national reports (Germany, Spain, France, Ireland, the Netherlands and the UK) point to the determining role of deteriorating health or growing dependence as regards entry into an institution. In Ireland, for example, more than half the old people in long-stay geriatric units are suffering from a chronic illness; in the Netherlands, according to the new regulations, admission is subject to evidence of ill-health.

Ill-health alone is rarely a sufficient ground for entry into an institution, which is usually co-determined by social circumstances. This is, for example, the case in 37% of admissions to geriatric units in Ireland, a proportion that rises to 60% of admissions to welfare homes, which were originally designed for people in need of care [O'Shea, 1991, pp 14, 15]. One of the main social reasons for admission to an institution, throughout Europe, seems to be the absence of

---

1   [Eingeschränkte Selbstversorgung]

    The coefficient is calculated by grouping 14 activities, such as making a telephone call, organising one's own consumption of medicines, being able to be left alone during the day, preparing food, washing, dressing, going to the toilet without help.

relatives, particularly a spouse or children, who can support the dependent older person in his or her own home or, as is still more common in the Member States in the Mediterranean region, who live with him or her. In the case of France, we know that the proportion of unmarried, childless old people is far higher among those in institutions than among those living in their own homes.

Another powerful social reason that leads people to enter an institution is the absence or inadequacy of domiciliary services, leaving old people with the simple alternative: family or institution. According to the Spanish report, illness and dependence are grounds for admissions of the very elderly in particular; leaving aside people who have a family and enough money to be able to stay in their own homes, loneliness and insufficient financial means are the major reasons for admissions of younger old people, and particularly women. The Portuguese report points to the fact that old people, and particularly old people living in an urban area, have no alternative but to enter an institution because they have no access to domiciliary services.

Future outlook

It is not uncommon for demographic forecasts (considerable increase in the number and percentage of the older elderly) and figures on the current proportion of elderly who are dependent (whose needs are barely being met by statutory and voluntary networks) to be combined, leading to the conviction that the number of old people and the number of dependent old people will increase in the same proportions. Thus, the German national report states "that we must expect the increasing percentage of the elderly population in the future to be matched by an increasing percentage of the sick elderly population". The Dutch report is less alarmist, stating that "the assumption that there will be a general improvement in old people's health is groundless in fact. As is now the case, a majority will enjoy relatively good health in the future. A minority will need special, individual attention and will be dependent on long-term care". The French report is the most cautious, or perhaps the most optimistic, in pointing to the numerous unknowns that make any extrapolation extremely precarious, but in speculating on the potential of medical developments.

5. Services for elderly people and family carers

Theory - Ideal - Reality

Theoretically, the solutions on offer when there is a loss of autonomy are three in number:

[] family
this means the provision of care by the spouse and/or (in the case of absence or impossibility) the descendant(s) or between siblings; a concerted effort by several members is not infrequent;

[] formal community care
these include a more or less diversified range of services, and function through paid professionals and/or volunteers (as for example more particularly in Ireland and the United Kingdom);

[] residential care
including hospitals fulfilling de facto or de jure the functions of shelter and care in the long term: in some cases (still very rare in the Community) in geriatric units specially designed for patients with chronic illness and other dependent elderly persons, but more frequently in general medical departments (where physicians will not usually have any special training in geriatric medicine).

A fourth solution could be added: informal provision of care by networks of neighbours. This can in fact play a decisive role in favour of staying at home, but according to the literature this remains, generally speaking, a rather marginal solution.

This tends to be limited to rather specific and sporadic services - as regards both the action performed and the duration of help - and to types of care which do not exceed a certain degree of responsibility.

(For example, a person living alone and suffering memory loss can be effectively supervised and supported by a neighbour, **if** that neighbour is operating above a *safety-net* provided by the family or by a specialist service.)

Ideally – and there is a certain consensus on this topic – these three (or four) approaches should co-exist and be developed in parallel, so that elderly people and their families are allowed a situation of **real choice**. Today only Denmark appears to be succeeding in what must be called quite an achievement.

In reality, the interaction between these three domains is not based upon the desires and needs of elderly people or their families, nor does it function according to the volume and types of care which families and elderly people need. It is significant that all degrees and categories of dependence can be found receiving care from the three sectors with an infinite variability of combinations creating considerable national, regional and local differences. Balances and imbalances between these three domains, in bare outline, are regulated as a function of socio-political choices (or the absence of these) and *of the ideology of the family*; these two are interdependent [Dieck, 1991: 445-448].

A principle

It appears that all Member States believe in the maxim of maintaining dependent elderly people at home; expectations as to the implementation of this principle fall between two extremes in the Community: giving responsibility to the family with a withdrawal (or non-involvement) of the State, or assumption of responsibility by the State with a **removal** of responsibility (but not a **withdrawal**) of the family.

Aids, allowances and services for elderly people and their families with a view to keeping dependent elderly persons at home seem to depend, in the first place, on expectations with regard to the family. Referring to the European research projects of the ACRE programme (*Age*

Care Research Europe), Anne Jamieson notes the very small amount of attention given to family carers in Denmark and Germany. In Denmark, no authority either individual or collective expects the family to provide care, because the responsibility for providing care is incumbent on the State and the State assumes this responsibility. In Germany, little attention is paid to the family carers by the socio- political decision-makers for quite another reason: "because they are seen to be performing their **duties**. Any acknowledgement of their existence through the provision of support or monetary compensation is seen as an erosion of a fundamental principle of welfare based on family responsibility" [Jamieson, 1991]: it is part of the *normal* duty of descendants, part of their *moral* and *ethic*al duty to take care of their father and mother [Dieck, 1991: 447]. The national report on Greece shows a similar expectation of the family on the part of the State, but what may be surprising here - because one is dealing with a rich welfare state - can be understandable in the context of a country which is much more disadvantaged on an economic and social level. Italy, Spain and Portugal also tend to expect that the principle of community care should be implemented by **the family.**

In the United Kingdom and in France, to a greater extent than in most other Member States, caring for carers is already advanced on the political agenda. It is broadly articulated in socio-political designs, and - admittedly in lesser proportions - forms part of certain socio-political practices. This does not prevent an ambiguous situation from prevailing in these two countries; what was found in the British report - summarised below - seems broadly to hold true at least for France. There is widespread agreement among the public in the United Kingdom: looking after older relatives is, within certain limits (which are however ill-defined) part of the responsibility of the descendants. At a conceptual level, there is a consensus between public opinion and political opinion, which tends to hold that the family needs to be supported by professionals. On the other hand, there is a contradiction between political practices and opinions, because they seem to reflect the idea that family care should be the norm and that the intervention of services should be limited to cases where the family is at the end of its resources, geographically too remote, or non-existent.

The differences between Member States such as the United Kingdom and France, as well as probably Belgium and the Netherlands and countries such as Greece as well as apparently Italy, reside in the fact that those in the first category have a commitment to a more equitable sharing of responsibilities between the family and the State; even if the implementation of this desire is slow, particularly on account of financing problems. In Greece this commitment is absent. In Germany, Spain and Portugal there is evidence of the first steps towards such a commitment but this is found only in parts of the country. In the developed welfare states **spouses** providing care, because they are elderly themselves, find it relatively easy to obtain assistance from professionals, unlike the younger carers.

It would appear that apart from Denmark, there is no country of the Community in which political opinion really manages to overcome the fear that a major opening of community care services to family carers might involve a withdrawal from responsibility on the part of the family. This fear persists - particularly in the minds of German politicians [Dieck, 1991: 448] - and it persists without proof. It persists despite the eloquent *counter-example* of Denmark, clearly shown by the findings of the ACRE programme: while it is true that the younger generation are less occupied in caring **for** their parents, it would be false to believe that they do not care **about** them. Quite the contrary is true: "It is possible that the stresses and strains of many people who are involved in mobilising the care system and in providing social support for their older relatives are underestimated and ignored by providers. Similarly, the real burden carried by spouses may not be sufficiently acknowledged in this system." [Jamieson, 1991]

Community care
Similarities and divergences in concepts

As regards the existence of services for community care in the strict sense - services which tend to be destined for elderly people - one may distinguish two groups of countries according to the extent and diversity of these services:

[] *Classic* welfare States which have developed a more or less extensive range of community care services: Germany, Belgium, Denmark, France, Netherlands, United Kingdom.

With the exception of Germany, a common feature of all of these is that they give priority to household help and home care, but one may observe differences in the priority given to one or other of these.[1]

Germany has developed household help to a very minor extent (2% of beneficiaries aged 65 or over, as against 8% in France),[2] but it has given priority (for institutional reasons [Dieck, 1991: 434]) for a long time to the delivery of meals[3].

---

1 Thus France has developed household help to a considerably greater degree, both because of local facilities for implementing it and for financial reasons. (The needs are not however covered, either as regards the number of beneficiaries, or as regards the number of hours provided [Jani-Le Bris, 1990b].)

2 The Danish beneficiaries of household help on a permanent basis represent, as a percentage of **households**: 13% aged between 67 and 74, 35% aged between 75 and 84, 63% aged 85 or older [Plovsing, 1991: 9].

3 This is a controversial decision in Germany because it is not based on proof that the needs match the extent of the supply and because, conversely, a number of studies prove the existence of needs in the area of household help. It is not uninteresting to note that the social services in France are more and more dubious about the supply of meals on wheels, and tending more and more to supply only people who are confined to their homes, because of its negative effects: for reasons of social relations and activities it is desirable to put pressure indirectly on elderly people to mobilise themselves to do their own shopping and be active in their kitchens.

It is necessary to emphasise for these countries that, in the first place, supply remains below demand and, in the second place, there are major regional and sometimes local disparities.

[]   The other Member States have developed this type of service to a very small extent, and only small beginnings can be seen here and there.

That is the case in **Ireland**, particularly on account of voluntary movements which are and are not linked to the Church.

In **Luxembourg** the situation seems to be improving: different community care services (home help, day centres, meals on wheels, etc.) have been developed since the later eighties, thanks to the success of the National Programmes for Elderly [Espace Social Européen, 1991: 146]. Nevertheless the 1992's National Programme still states (supported by a national study) that "the intermediary infrastructure (community care services) is rather non-existent" [Eberhard et al, 1992: 11]. Furthermore it is stressed that there are important gaps in residential care too (namely insufficient number of beds and inadequacies to the needs of the elderly).

A socio-gerontological policy in favour of community care is emerging in **Italy** - especially in northern Italy - which goes along with the generalised objective of the welfare state to stave off admission to a residential institution, ... perhaps bypassing the stage (through which the Danish, Dutch or Luxembourgeois systems have passed) of concentrating efforts on creating institutions.

But while a number of structures are planned, the existence of services is fragmentary and isolated [Facchini, 1991]. This same author points out that this type of service is also "extremely inadequate for the needs and frequently reserved for a very small minority which benefits from a few hours here and there" [ibid.].

In **Spain** and **Portugal** the situation is thought to be comparable to that which obtains in Italy. Some regional governments in Spain are setting up community care services which are, as yet, fragmentary and, as the development in Portugal is only beginning, it is mostly happening in towns and cities.

Greece appears to be the worst served in this area; in addition, there are major deficiencies in the hospital system. Three hospitals in Athens provide home services for people (of all age groups) suffering from cancer and living with their families. But the national report also mentions a large number of islands and regions where neither hospitals nor home care can be found. As regards household tasks, the employment of a domestic cleaner is quite common in towns **if** financial resources permit.[1] Despite this, Greek social policy has developed approximately 250 KAPI, day centres for the elderly[2]; their primary aim is recreational, but they may well go on to extend their activities (essentially voluntary) to household help. A small number of local authorities had set up programmes of home help which have had to be discontinued after the government removed the financing, with the exception of a programme financed under the third European programme against poverty.

During the last ten years, Spain, Greece, Italy and Portugal have mostly set up *indirect* community care services, probably having preventive effects as they promote social belonging and integration, and combat boredom and loneliness. On the one hand, these involve recreational centres and cultural and leisure activities, etc., while on the other hand they involve the organisation of social holidays. (It may be noted that the more northerly countries have been running such activities for a long time, to complement their other services.)

---

1 The use of the services of a housekeeper is also not exceptional in Germany.

2 Scattered all over the national territory, in towns, in the countryside, on the islands.

Like other socio-gerontological measures, these actions are aimed at elderly people, but bring benefits, through them, to the carers, who are given breaks in the caring situation.

Although it is obvious, we may note the importance of housing conditions for community care, whether this is made available by the family or by the social services, whether the elderly person is living alone or with others. Restricted space and overcrowding in cases of co-residence, the poor condition of the housing, its deterioration, an awkward situation on an upper storey in a building with no lift, a lack of sanitary and household equipment all of these are elements which limit the prospects for domiciliary care; they also limit the pleasure of living there.

[] 23% of Spaniards aged over 84 live on at least the fourth floor (with no lift) [Perez Ortiz, 1991: 21].

[] **Lack** of facilities and equipment in a percentage of households where the head of household is aged 65 or older:

	Spain [Perez Ortiz, 1991: 21]	Ireland [O'Shea, 1991: 65]
Proportion without:		
indoor WC	51	30
cold water	1	15
hot water	24	36
washing machine[1]	18	65
refrigerator	.	27

[] The lack of a telephone affects 76% of people aged 65 and over in Ireland (same basis and sources as above) as against 10% in France [Christine and Samy, 1988].

---

1 By way of comparison two French figures may be mentioned: approximately 20% without a washing machine, and about 3% without a refrigerator [Christine and Samy, 1988].

Spain [Perez Ortiz, 1991: 21, 22] and Ireland [O'Shea, 1991: 9, 10] have now set up programmes to rehabilitate old housing stock and build new social housing units. Hygiene and comfort conditions do not merely determine the limits of community care, they regulate the quality of life.

Italy. A man aged seventy. He lives in a two-room dwelling which he shares with his family. No electricity, no sanitary facilities. Diseases have been heaped one on the other, he can barely move any more. If he had a bed, he would be bedridden. He spends his days in an old armchair which serves him as a bed at night.

How many comparable cases can we find in the Community?

Institutions: *living* spaces?

Whatever the Member State involved, whatever the social class, whatever the age (apart from extremely old people in one or two countries), the population living in an institution constitutes a minority: the highest rates found (which are exceptional) are as follows: 46% of 90-year-old Danes and 50% of "the oldest"[1] Belgians.[2] (See Table 12.)

The author of the Spanish research report explains: "The low percentage of old people in residential homes is evidence of the traditional dislike of such institutions and the significant role played by the family." Indeed, the causes of the low rates of institutionalisation show considerable diversity and difference according to the socio-gerontological context of the different countries. What seems most important, is the hostility to residential care which is ubiquitous in Europe. It is extremely rare that entering an institution is taken as a plan for life; rarely chosen, but used as a last resort, this is often

---

1   No further details.

2   One may reasonably suppose that certain sub-groups, such as widowed women aged 85 or older without children, reach rates of over 50% in some countries.

the last straw in a series of social failures. Curiously, even if the quality of a residential institution is a source of real well-being, the dislike persists[1]. **The potential carer must confront this context of widespread** rejection of institutional care when **managing the loss of autonomy in an older parent.** However, the Danish experience of high-quality establishments seems to show that descendants (and perhaps even spouses) can accept the situation without anxiety or guilt when a family member enters these institutions.

Under the pressure of demography on the one hand, and pressure from problems posed by caring for dependent people (both on account of their large number and on account of their considerable longevity) on the other hand, the countries of the Community have tended for several years to increase their residential care capacity.

In Italy, there was a growth of 50% between the 1950s and the end of the 1980s, although this remained below the level of increase in the number of people aged 70 or over [Facchini, 1991]. The Spanish, Portuguese and British reports indicate increases in residential capacity proportional to the increase in the elderly population; developments in France have been roughly similar. In Ireland [O'Shea, 1991: 4, 47] and the Netherlands, the rates of residential care have been constant for a number of years. With the exception of the Iberian countries (and possibly Luxembourg and Ireland) this pattern reflects the application of policies for domiciliary care. At its extreme in Denmark, the law forbids the creation of new residential establishments and social policy for the elderly aims to secure a *drastic* reduction in the rate of residential care.

---

1   The high quality of Danish institutions is recognised [Plovsing, 1991: 8] and yet, just like other Europeans, Danes declare their clear preference for living at home. The results of a French survey are similar: retired people who were questioned (in large numbers) defined their concept of an ideal residence for elderly people; but when they were questioned at the end about themselves entering such an establishment, which they themselves had seen as ideal, the number of positive responses came to only 1% [Jani-Le Bris, 1990a].

Is it unrealistic to hope that countries with major gaps in both sectors – residential care and community care services (Spain, Greece, Italy, Ireland, Portugal) – might create a social policy for the elderly which avoids the excessive development of institutional care?

Another aspect to be considered may be summed up in the question: institutions with a **social** purpose or institutions with a **medical** purpose? Denmark has given its answer, but what is the position elsewhere? From Germany [KDA, 1991: 4], from France and from the Netherlands [Knapen, 1991: 11], it appears that the boundaries between the two categories have become more and more fluid on account of changing demand: *applicants* are getting older and older[1], and more importantly are becoming more and more dependent and frail[2]; these latter characteristics are today a necessary condition for admission into a residential institution in the Netherlands.

Although – based upon knowledge of the situation in France – the great majority of dependent people do not need much medical care but simply medical supervision, paramedical care, and *aids for living*, a number of establishments in different countries are unable to cope with caring for dependent people, because they have an exclusively social orientation. The French sheltered housing schemes are an eloquent example of this[3]. It is obvious that adapting housing conditions to the needs of different types of dependence while, at the same time,

---

1   Average age of entry in Belgium: 82 years old.

2   It is significant that approximately 20% of Germans in a residential institution on any given day are staying for a very short time: they die relatively soon after admission [KDA, 1991:5].

3   Planned during the 1970s as a solution to the housing problems of elderly people, the clients had to be in good health to get into them. Where a dependent condition arose which exceeded the capacities of the community care services, the person involved had to go into another type of institution. Some of these establishments do not wish, or are not able, to adapt to the new type of demand and have problems in filling their places.

providing access to community care services avoids (or at least delays) entry into a residential establishment and consequently reduces demand. Towards the northern part of the Community, in particular, numerous examples prove this.

New kinds of home and residential care, halfway between traditional individual housing and residential institutions, are beginning to emerge in more than one Member State. There are multiple advantages: satisfaction both of the people living there and of their families, social integration into a district or a village, lower construction and running costs than those of residential institutions.

Some examples:

[] Wohngemeinschaften (residential communities) in Germany. There is a wide variety of these, they can be formal or informal, and they are often founded on the principle of mutual help, especially those which also include young people. [Metz, Dierl, 1984].

[] Ordinary apartments from the social rented housing stock, renovated and adapted to the specific requirements of handicap, in Germany, in France [Jani-Le Bris, 1991] and, in a large-scale development, in Denmark [Plovsing, 1991: 8, 9, 10]. The proximity between them makes it easy to secure help from assistance services and to remain in ones own district.

[] Sheltered collective apartments in France; these are small units integrated into the urban texture, with about twelve elderly people living together [Jani-Le Bris, ibid.]. One special type exists: the "Cantou"[1]; it specialises in taking in old people suffering from dementia [Fondation de France, 1988].

---

1 This expression borrowed from the "langue d'oc" designates the hearth.

[] Small constructions in rural areas of Britain and France. (Rehabilitating and adapting farms where agriculture is no longer carried on might also be a useful way of providing residential care, especially where dwellings are scattered over the countryside.)

[] Foster care in substitute families, in Germany, Ireland, France, the United Kingdom.

Leaving aside situations where there are dramatic deficiencies, as can be found particularly in Greece,[1] and with the apparent exception of Denmark, all Member States face major problems in the institutional sector. The efforts undertaken by some of them, particularly with a view to improving the quality of residential care, are only bearing fruit slowly.

---

1   This is characterised by inadequacies on the health and hospital front: a chronic shortage of hospital beds, paramedical personnel, residential establishments for elderly people who, in the absence of other solutions, stay in overcrowded hospitals; absence of geriatric services; lack of hospitals on the islands and in a number of regions.

CARING AND CARERS

Solidarity - duty of spouses - duty of children - duty of a wife - moral choice - conscience - social recognition - social pressure - affection - gratitude - generosity - giving oneself - sympathy - hatred - suffering - isolation - solitude - determination - dignity - sadness - depression - shame - guilt - search for love - search for forgiveness - anguish - despair - uncertainty - instability - demoralisation - hell - loss of identity - devotion - abnegation - bondage - self-discipline - patience - maturing - anger - revenge - violence - revolt - cries - tears - conflicts - fighting - power struggle - powerlessness - mourning - resignation - destiny - death.

Selfishness is conspicuous by its absence.

1. Introduction

The evidence is there: not all elderly people, even when they have reached a very advanced age, are dependent - which of us has not met that old lady described by Gillian Parker as "robust, active (...) in her eighties acting as the lynchpin in a family support network"? [Parker 1985: 11]

This second part of the report could however allow one to suppose this not to be the case as it concerns mostly people with heavy dependency; the present section could, more particularly, allow one to suppose that elderly people **receiving assistance from their families** are all badly affected by disability, and that their helpers are consequently all involved in situations of extreme difficulty. In fact, this is far from being the case. What happened was that social research, relatively recent in this area[1], had as its main objective to bring out and to have recognised the productivity of families in this area, identifying the weight of what this implies for carers, and emphasising the supports which these people need in order to lighten the volume and burden of the assistance which they take on. It therefore fitted in with the logic of these objectives to target the research on the most heavily affected groups[2].

As regards the decision to become a carer, the process towards an assumption of heavy responsibilities is usually slow and gradual, just as the process of losing autonomy is slow and gradual. Years can go by during which interventions remain limited; the hardest thing to put up with during this stage could be the underlying worry about the future, which is willingly consigned to the unconscious: *what to do if the condition becomes serious?*

---

1   In Germany, Belgium, Britain or France, for example, research on family carers has mostly developed from the 1980s onwards.

2   The same is true of almost all the 134 semi-directive interviews carried out in this research for the European Foundation, in six Member States: Germany, Spain, France, Greece, Netherlands, Portugal.

It seems important to emphasise at the outset how immensely complex is the context of family care. The caring situation has many facets, as it takes in almost all aspects of life; it encompasses and concerns the individual in all his or her psychological complexity (in fact, at least two individuals); it is a relationship and this is rooted in decades of married life for some people, in childhood for others; it is anchored in the uses and customs of every society, in social, family and religious culture. Every caring situation has its own history, every situation forms part of an individual progress as well as part of the history of a family.

The relevance of any international comparison lies in the identification of differences and similarities. In this second chapter we shall try to contribute to this process, but it will be found that on more than one point the questions remain more numerous than the answers.

The results of the six qualitative studies (carried out in Germany, Spain, France, Greece, the Netherlands and Portugal) are integrated into what follows.

2. Who are the carers?

Gaps in knowledge on carer profiles

Having regard to the absence of surveys based on representative national samples in most member States, information on the characteristics of carers is incomplete. The information which exists normally derives from small samples of an unrepresentative kind, linked moreover to one town or one region; certain pieces of information exclude spouses as carers, while others draw no distinction on the basis of relationship to the dependent person; others deal only with carers for people with a mental illnes, or a specific physical condition.

Sex

The various sources are unanimous in finding a predominance of females: being a carer is something for women. In fact, without being **really** false in the *general European situation*, this statement needs to be differentiated, at least in relation to the type of carer involved (which is done in a number of research reports).

A majority of carers - which certainly excludes Spain and perhaps other carers in southern Europe - **is made up of spouses** (for example, 75% according to a German survey; 49% according to a Belgian survey) [Nijkamp et al., 1991:92][1]. Among the **spouses** acting as carers,

there are **as many men as women** in Britain, Ireland and the Netherlands, and it appears likely that a relative balance between the two **sexes** also exists in other countries situated in the centre and north of the Community. (We shall return to the specific situation in Spain, see section 3 below.) It is known for a number of these Member States (Germany, Belgium, France, Ireland, Netherlands, United Kingdom) that male carers are usually the husband, and thus more rarely the son or the son-in-law of the recipient of care.

On the other hand, among **descendants, female predominance is undoubted** in all Member States: daughters and, generally to a smaller proportion, daughters-in-law, form a large majority of this group.

Marital status

Having regard to what has just been stated, the large proportion of married people, taking all carers together, is not surprising (for example, 73% in Germany, 67% in Ireland). But here again, the distinction between spouses and descendants is necessary as, while the total number in the former category are married by definition - and

---

1   It is clear that these figures only have an indicative value, as everything depends on the definition of what level has to be reached before the spouse can be considered as a carer. A number of studies underline the difficulties of spouses - especially wives - in recognising themselves in this role, sometimes even when there is a situation of heavy dependency.

54

they constitute the majority – the probability for daughters and daughters-in-law, in particular, of becoming widows increases seriously in their later fifties. Thus, the constellation of mother and daughter-carer, both widowed, is apparently far from being exceptional all over Europe, but perhaps more particularly in southern Europe.

Never married people also appear to make up a significant proportion, especially if they have never left the parental home[1]. This gives rise for example to the situation of an *old bachelor* living with his

widowed mother, a constellation which led one French demographer to ask slightly ironically   which side of the equation the dependency lies [Audirac, 1985: 49].

This information is still only indicative; the marital status of carers other than spouses is not reliably known for general populations. This lack of information limits any quantified analysis of the possible specificities of different marital situations.

It may for example be supposed that unmarried people are more likely to be destined (or **choose** to be destined) for the role of carer, and that the absence of family responsibilities facilitates this task for them; but it may also be supposed that these people are more vulnerable to the negative consequences of the carers role given their double risk of isolation due to their personal situation and to this role. But these are only suppositions.

Age

This characteristic of carers is also insufficiently known, Here, more than ever, the distinction between descendants and spouses caring for people is necessary if one wishes to evaluate the *care for carers* – and the bare information that ages are spread out between 20 and over 85 do

---

1   13% of German carers and 23% of Irish carers are never married. This latter percentage rises to 61% among male carers; we may recall the special demographic feature in Ireland, which is the *historically* low marriage rate.

not provide much assistance. There is some more precise information in existence, but this is still inadequate to comprehend the real situation and advance a European comparison.

The age of German carers is divided as follows:

> 90% under 50
> 32% between 50 and 64
> 24% between 65 and 74
> 22% between 75 and 84
> 3% 85 or over

[Thiede, 1988: 253].

While some authors of the national reports have been able to supply information on age, taken together they are insufficient to allow valid deductions to be made as regards the possible influence of this variable, closely linked to the health and hence to the capacity to provide care, especially over the long term. The need to know the breakdown by age of the different types of family carers substantiates the need for surveys based on large representative national samples which exist only in the UK.

Health

Again, there is a deficit in knowledge of this aspect, particularly for identifying deterioration caused by caring.

As for **spouses**, the **similarities between the carer and the recipient of care** are a decisive element according to all the research findings - a fact which is often true of siblings too: the two people belong to the same age-group, and the older the carer is, the more he or she is exposed to risks of physical and psychological effects. The woman's age, which is generally lower than her husband's, is often counterbalanced by the higher level of invalidity among women. Thus the situation of elderly couples is often characterised by mutual support which operates in a delicate balance and negotiates a slow deterioration of the two, one propping up the other in terms of what each one is still able to bear, mobilised by their fear of being obliged to enter an institution. In this type of relationship the principal carer, if one exists, is difficult to determine.

No Member State knows the scale of this situation of mutual dependency, any more than the number and proportion of other combinations of health on the part of the carer and cared-for are known.

As regards **descendants**, information about their health is even less reliable, and hypotheses are difficult to state given the large spread of ages among carers. Even though there is great interest in the impact of caring on the carer's health very little is well established.

Co-residence

Large proportions of carers and recipients of care are believed to reside under the same roof. It appears that co-residence

[]   is the predominant model in the southern countries, despite the changes taking place particularly in the urban environment. The Greek report underlines a fact which is probably true for other country areas (as for example in France): the shared nature of buildings and hence the proximity of the dwellings of grown-up children and their aged parents often makes it difficult to determine whether there is co-residence or not;

[]   is usual when the carers are spouses;

[]   is more frequent among descendants providing care when the recipient of care is very dependent.

Carers in paid employment

To the extent that existing research generally concerns people in a very dependent situation, the recipients of care who have been taken into consideration are generally rather old; **spouses** providing care while still carrying on their work activity are consequently often excluded by being beyond normal retirement age. However, in the perspective of caring for carers, one partner in couples aged between 55 and 70 may very well be still in paid employment.

The combination of paid work and a carer's role does not constitute the predominant model in the Community, not even in its central or northern countries (although the Netherlands, where nearly all descendant carers are at home, certainly stands at one extreme). The combination of the two situations seems however to be not infrequent; across all age groups in Belgium about one carer in four is employed, in Ireland they represent 16% among female carers and 42% among male carers, and in Germany respectively 16% and 32%.

Women seem to be more willing than men to abandon their career so as to take care of a family member. According to some French works, it would appear that the presence of several reasons for giving up work is not rare (unsatisfying job, dismissal or risk of dismissal, possibility of early retirement, etc.). According to a German survey, one woman in ten has stopped work because she is taking charge of a family member. [Thiede, 1986]. (The report of this survey does not specify either the age of these women or the age of the recipients of care, so the latter could include children.)

Duration of care

Data from three Member States support the hypothesis that care tends to be a long-term undertaking: admittedly between 40% and 50% have been carers for a maximum of *only* five years, but to what extent are they still at the beginning? Twenty-six per cent of British carers have been caring for between five and nine years, while more than one-third of Belgians have been caring for between six and fifteen years. A quarter of carers in the United Kingdom have a very long-term situation (ten years or more), while the same is true of 12% in Belgium (fifteen years or more).

Several national reports emphasise the fragmentary aspect of any assessment of duration at a given moment; on the one hand, if the carer is able to date the beginning of his or her intervention, he or she can in fact indicate the time which has elapsed subsequently, but will in no way be able to predict the amount of time left in the future. On the other hand, this evaluation does not take account of successive or contemporaneous caring roles – often connected with the model of the traditional family. Now, it is very common for women in particular to have taken on – either inadvertently or purely because they were born female – a career of caring: "Often they had cared for more than one person in their lifetime. For example, in one study it was established

combination of child and **mother**. The recipient of care from a son (or son-in-law) is thus likely to be his mother. Since the care which is needed involves the body and touching, this may give rise to anxiety around the problem of incest. To what extent would a situation of a son helping a mother be affected by the taboo linked to this? The absence of this taboo between married couples might explain why there is no barrier for men to become carers for their wives. Such concerns are not well researched but may be a factor in the observable tendency for sons to look after their fathers, while daughters are more likely to take charge of their mothers (although this latter tendency may also be connected with demographic circumstances). It may also be an issue in the apparently widespread refusal of sons providing care to get involved in the hygiene needs of their mothers (or their difficulty in bringing their mothers to the toilet). Undoubtedly, daughters experience the same taboo with regard to their fathers, and several semi-directive interviews in France reveal the revulsion which they feel every time they are forced to look after the intimate bodily needs of their father or father-in-law. On the whole though - and largely for demographic reasons - daughters unlike the sons, are generally involved in helping a parent of the same sex.

[] As emphasised by the French report among others, any care situation is in the first place a caring **relationship.** The reasons for any intervention by sons involve an analysis of son/mother relationships, which are fundamentally different from daughter/mother relationships.

[] Unlike the choice, the actual assumption of a care responsibility by sons is undertaken with a sense of *interior distance*; women (whether wife or daughter) take this on with strong emotional implications; a certain consensus exists in this regard. Sons generally remain far from the very high *psychological cost*[1] of daughters, as well as avoiding the

---

1 Self-denial, guilt feelings, loss of identity, marital conflict, anguish, etc., are more likely to be experienced by women.

psychosomatic consequences. These *male* forms of emotional resistance may perhaps explain two other significant phenomena of gender-related behaviour: on the one hand, men are sooner to establish their limits in relation to what they are prepared to bear, and thus less frequently take on heavily dependent parents; on the other hand, sons appear to have less difficulty in deciding that parents should go into an old peoples home.

But it should be emphasised that the distance which sons maintain in relation to assistance does not preserve them from the pain and sorrow deriving from the physical or psychological deterioration of their parents, and from their death.

[] It follows that men are often better than women at preserving themselves in the care situation, and maintaining their free time, networks of relationships outside the family, and professional life and hobbies. The almost complete isolation which one often finds in the daughter/mother combination in cases of heavy dependency would appear to be rather rare among male carers (whether sons or husbands).

It should be emphasised that, paradoxically, sons receive more assistance then daughters, and their maintenance of free time is based on shared interventions by women in their immediate surroundings, but also by professional backup services.

[] Some non-material benefits appear to be conferred on sons and to a much smaller extent on daughters who care for parents. With regard to social values, daughters who care are just doing their duty and any departure from this social norm is met with disapproval, even in their own eyes: they tend to feel guilty the moment they think of themselves, for example by taking some time off. The situation of sons in a caring situation is completely different: the social norms give them merit and praise for their action and their social circle (including the women) willingly sympathises with them and admires them.

[] Male carers have little problem in delegating various tasks to professionals (or other people from outside) and thus in accepting help; women are more likely to have difficulties with this.

However, a new type of female carer, more *healthy* from a psychological point of view, seems to be advancing: the woman who knows that her balance - not least her balance as a carer - depends on her occupational activity. In order to maintain this, she is willing to delegate; it is through her tendency to feel guilty about that, however, that she is different from men.

[] Sons in a caring situation are generally concentrated on tasks and assistance of a social kind (visiting the parents, keeping them company, keeping an eye on them, taking them for walks, doing administrative tasks, looking after their money, doing the shopping, etc.) and are less likely to do housework. As far as possible they refuse to become involved with hygiene requirements or personal care.

3. Decisions - Motivations - Limits

As emphasised in the Greek report, if there is to be a real decision, there has to be **choice**: choice between a range of possibilities which are presented by the availability or *goodwill* of another potential carer, the proper functioning and accessibility of community care services and, lastly, the existence of residential homes of a high quality and reasonable cost.

As already indicated the public *supply* of home services and residential accommodation is very poorly developed in the four southern Member States. Even in those more northerly states which have been spending considerable resources for a number of decades on their geriatric/social policies, a situation of genuine choice is rarely guaranteed, except perhaps in Denmark. The *European carer* is thus rarely placed in a situation of genuine choice.

This absence of choice – including for other reasons which will be mentioned later – is ever-present as a leitmotif in the motivation of carers.

Becoming and remaining a carer

There are two main ways of entering into a caring situation – all national reports underline this – either through a slow, creeping process, or following a sudden incident. The categorisation of carers according to the way they began caring is generally unknown[1], but it appears that care following a sudden incident is relatively infrequent.

The **creeping process** is slow and gradual, generally related to the slow progression of loss of autonomy (poor sight becomes blindness; memory problems become disorientation and incontinence).

> *My mother always needed a bit of help, and I gave her more when she needed more. (Netherlands)*
> *... and then you find you're no longer calling once a week for fun, ... you're visiting more often. (Netherlands)*

The beginnings of care are thus difficult or impossible to date. Another characteristic often obtains: people become carers without noticing, without taking any conscious decision, sometimes even without identifying themselves with the *status* of carers, because care is so natural and integrated into their daily habits. This process is evidently favoured by co-residence and is thus particularly frequent between spouses.

A **sudden incident** has three basic origins: an illness or accident (fracture of the hip, stroke, heart attack, etc.), after which the older person is cared for at home; widowhood; and the *resignation* or death of the previous carer.

---

1   Only Ireland presents figures identifying 79% by a slow, creeping process.

In these cases, the beginnings of care are easy to date and the decision is taken in a (more) conscious manner, although not necessarily with more choice.

It is not infrequent – and this seems to be true of all countries – for there to be, if not negotiation, at least some consultation between brothers and sisters usually giving rise to mentioning at least the question of residential care. Since the cases presented here are dealing with carers, the residential care solution has not been chosen, or is not available, or possibly accepted as an extreme solution to be applied later. It is generally at this point that the principal carer is either designated or steps forward. It is easy to imagine that this sort of context is more likely to produce an emotional decision, rather than a decision taken with mature consideration and clearsightedness: this is a crisis situation, people find themselves shocked by what has happened, distracted, worried about their parent, but also worried about themselves and they do not necessarily have enough information about other solutions to measure the situation objectively. It is also easy to imagine that this context may be conflict-laden.

The general tendency appears to be that this type of consultation is held *behind closed doors*: **excluding** the elderly person, sometimes not even knowing what he or she would prefer. It seems likely that if the recipient of care were involved in the discussion, many later conflicts would be avoided, both for the carer and for the recipient of care, because the context would be clearer for everybody; but for that to happen, the potential carers would need to recognise their limits openly, and the recipient of care would need to be able to listen *generously* to them.

Clearly, of course, there are also *intermediate ways of entry*, such as the interruption of the imperceptible process by a sudden incident, for example an intensive but temporary period of care (crisis, illness) which one day becomes definitive, or a gradual decision to take an elderly dependent relative out of the residential institution to which he or she had previously been consigned.

Another phenomenon which has emerged in a number of national reports is the fact that a majority of carers do not really understand what they are getting involved in. The Irish report gives precise figures: 28% reported that they had no idea of what taking care would involve, and 39% had imagined a smaller burden than what actually happened. This problem of *unawareness* is absent when this type of care forms part of the history of a family or an individual - meaning that the carer is not getting involved in care for the first time, or that at a younger age he or she saw his or her mother doing the same thing.

Lastly, there is also the case of the carer - perhaps more common in southern Europe - who has never worried for a moment about what the care situation will or could mean in his or her life.

This phenomenon of *unawareness* frequently goes hand in hand with an absence of knowledge and experience of heavy dependency. A large number of carers, wherever they may be, *make do and learn on the job*. For male carers, lack of experience in care is compounded by inexperience in household matters; this is particularly the case with men who belong to a social setting which in no way gave them this type of function, because it was typically a female responsibility - cases which are more widespread still in the south.

> *I've never been involved with all those household things, I've never got involved in washing women. I don't know how to make a household work. (Spain)*

> *I always have the impression of doing things badly, that a woman would do better. I'm a man, and men are not brought up to be housemaids. (Spain)*

To remain in Spain, there are many Spanish women (and certainly many elsewhere) who have consciously built up the power and experience of a mistress of the household, built up over long apprenticeship, women who are well used to looking after other people.

What motivations lead exactly to becoming, and then remaining a carer? This area is obviously one of the most complex ones, and as the British report emphasises, there is often an amalgam of reasons. It is affected by the traditions of a country, the social norms, the stage of evolution in changing family structures, the concept of lifestyle and the history of each individual.

The notion of **duty**, in its many aspects, is mentioned in all the national reports. It is perhaps the predominant motivation - it is certainly the most powerful one. It prevails even where there is no attachment or affection to the recipient of care; the weight of duty is reinforced in societies where filial duty is accepted as law or where social structures for care of the elderly are inadequate, and this does not only happen in the southern countries. On the basis of a first reading of the national reports, there is an impression of a north/south separation in the concept of duty, in the sense that in the south - anchored in the model of a traditional family - duty had the character of **social** norms and laws, while in the north it was a **moral** duty. However, the research findings indicate that these two *categories of duty* are tangled up with each other (in a variable fashion according to the individual, family and social context) and the boundaries between the two forms of duty are fluid.

The rules obtaining in rural Spanish society (or at least Catalan society), may be exclusive to just this society and represent a model which has seen its day in the rest of modern Europe.

Nevertheless, for present purposes, the interest of this model resides in its *purity* which leads to an understanding of the strength of the notion of duty as a reason for becoming and remaining a carer; it also helps in understanding the impact of distant roots of behaviours and attitudes of *European women* faced with the dependence of elderly parents - behaviours and attitudes which some people would call anachronistic in modern society.

[] **Rural society in Spain** (Catalonia)

Any decision to take care of dependent relatives has to do with the **intrinsic duty of a woman and a daughter**. This derives from the status, rights and obligations of the wife of the inheriting son, which take effect on the wedding day, leaving her **alone** responsible for all members of the family group (in co-residence) needing care, whatever their age and family relationship. The marriage of the inheriting son sets his mother free from the same rights and obligations which she bore in her time: there is a transfer of power in the household to the daughter-in-law. Because of the *matter at stake* - the inheritance - it is duty to her **husband** that makes her operate in this way, because if she fails to do so he is disinherited. This is the context in which we must understand that taking care of elderly relatives is seen as natural and as an integral task in family life.

It should be noted that the assumption of responsibility for the **father-in-law** - *absolute master* of the family group because he holds the purse-strings - begins the day that the daughter-in-law enters the house, without him having to be dependent: it is her business to look after his domestic needs (clothes, food, etc.) and of course to look after him in case of illness and dependence. She does the same for her mother-in-law as regards care. That is what explains the absence of caring spouses, female or male.

As a girl, the daughter-in-law was educated to this form of life, and it would never cross her mind to challenge it. She knows that this life is a tacit component of marriage, due to inheritance.

In the absence of an inheriting son, one of the daughters, preferably the youngest who then has to remain unmarried (or else a widowed daughter) is designated by the father - she will be the inheritor, and she takes on the powers over the household including responsibility for all members of the family group. This designation of an unmarried daughter is linked to her financial and social dependence on her parents.

This model shows the separation but also the sharing of roles and entitlements between men and women. Despite the submission which the daughter-in-law owes to her father-in-law, it would be obviously incorrect to associate her with the image of a *sacrificed woman*: as the **mistress** of the household, she has a high degree of power, including power over men in the family group. Other compensations, which are not negligible, can be found in the social prestige and recognition which she gains in her social circle: *she is a respectable woman, she is an honourable and proper woman.*

[] **Urban Spanish society** (Barcelona)

The prevailing set of phenomena make the context very different here, totally restructuring the provision of care for the elderly. Inheritances are less frequent and less substantial. The father/father-in-law is consequently stripped of his social power, urban housing does not offer the same space as rural housing, which rules out the co-residence of a number of lateral and descendant families, a number of women carry on wage-earning activities and have achieved financial independence.

Thus, the caring spouse is frequent among elderly couples, and the caring son is not exceptional, but the woman - daughter or daughter-in-law - remains in the first rank if there are difficulties with her parents or parents-in-law, due to widowhood, illness, or the loss of physical or psychological autonomy.

The duty or **social pressure** which can be found in other forms in Greece, Italy and Portugal on account of their fundamental attachment to a traditional family model, survives in the *modern world*. To state it in simplified form, a family (and that effectively means the woman) loses prestige in the eyes of others if it does not take care of its elderly dependent members, and gains prestige if it complies with the *rule*.

Moral duty may have different forms and origins; those which were cited most frequently in the national reports were:

[]   Giving back what you received.

> *For me, it's something normal to do. She is my mother, she always took care of me. When the time comes that she needs help, the children have got to look after their mother. (Netherlands)*

[]   Avoiding guilt, so as to have a good conscience, to escape from shame, to maintain esteem (of oneself and of others).

[]   The promise given (sometimes dragged out) seems not to be mentioned often as a motivation in the existing works on carers; proof of this is that none of the national reports alludes to it in the desk research portion, but it does emerge in the qualitative studies. The diversity of content and provenance[1] suggest that this is not only a marginal practice.

The examples:

[]   The father on his deathbed asks his children to look after their mother. (Germany)
An analogous case is particularly painful: an only daughter finds the same request being made by her dying father after looking after him for twenty-two years at the cost of great sacrifices. We questioned her as a carer for her mother, whom she does not like, in her twenty-fourth year of providing care. (France)

[]   After the suicide of his wife, a man accepts her plea (in the letter that she left) to take charge of his parents-in-law until their death. (France)

---

1   Germany, France and Greece - we exclude here the decisive role of inheritance in Spain, because this is not a moral obligation.

[] An elderly husband makes the following will: the couple's property will be divided in equal portions between their children, on condition that they all take care of the survivor. (Greece) Analogous examples were encountered among the German and French carers[1].

Spouses providing care have an intrinsic motivation which generally suffices by itself: lifelong marital solidarity, as they got married *for better or for worse*. All national reports mention this; it is therefore a motivation which is widespread in the Community, at least in generations of elderly couples (although we do not know how many couples separate because one of them becomes dependent).

Our married life was wonderful (...) years of harmony; it goes without saying that one of us would support the other in case of illness. What's going on here is for love and affection. For my part, the care which I am giving is part of my tasks ... we have never been separated for a long time. (Germany)

We have been married for forty years. We have shared everything, joys and worries. Each of us has good points and bad points. We are Catholic and we are obliged to look after each other. (Netherlands)

I would feel ashamed if I put him into a home. No, I won't do that. The president and the priest said to me: "You're going to kill yourself!" "What do you mean!" I answered them, "as long as I live I'll look after him as best I can. If I die, I won't see what's happening any more, and you can do what you like." (Greece)

One motivation, raised in quotations from some carers who were interviewed; seems rarely to be included in other research: the influence of European people's roots in Christianity. For example, love

---

1   This type of will provision was very frequent in some French regions; we do not know if such arrangements are still widespread in our own day.

of one's neighbour and help for others "are given considerable value in the gospels through the exemplary actions of Jesus". [Rosenmayr, 1988:9]

Positive and real feelings - affection, love, tenderness and even pity - also contribute to motivations, it should be emphasised, in the knowledge, however, if only through reading several national reports (the Greek and the British reports, for example) that these sentiments in no way represent a condition for taking care, and also knowing that *Love is not enough* [Bettelheim, 1970, title of book]. Other motivations which obviously exist in all countries and which belong to this same category, include strong links and family solidarity between brothers and sisters, or sincere gratitude to one's parents **without** implying the notion of **duty** in return to pay back a debt.

One motivation is ever-present in all Member States; the **stated wish to prevent a relative from being taken into residential care.** This refusal has two concomitant and interactive sources: in relating worries about the negative image of residential institutions, and loss of esteem, both in one's own eyes and among one's social circle: placing a relative in an institution often generates shame and guilt, even in the long term, and is seen as abandonment and failure[1]. These effects can be such that the former carer does not dare to visit the former recipient of care (which leads the staff of residential institutions to believe that families abandon their aged relatives just at the point when they need them most).

Several **circumstances** or **practical reasons** appear conducive to bearing care responsibilities of which four appear in all national reports:

---

1   The need to justify the placing, sometimes years later, is important. In the French semi-directive interviews, every carer who had placed an elderly relative in a residential institution launched into a long speech to justify this action, even if the recipient of care was in a very advanced state of dementia.

[]   co-residence for a long time
a child who has never left the parental home; integration into the single-parent home of a widowed and autonomous grandmother, on an exchange basis, etc.;

[]   geographical proximity of the carer and the recipient of care;

[]   absence of structures providing assistance at home and/or in residential care;

[]   financial cost of placement in residential care too expensive for the low income of the family. This reason seems to be most frequent in Greece, and may be reinforced by the fact that the carer, in the absence of an independent income, lives on the pension of the recipient of care.

The **reasons that people continue** to provide care appear generally identical to those which led to the establishment of that situation.

The current state of knowledge appears insufficiently developed to understand where, why and how changes in motivation to care take place. Let us take the example of worsening dependence; this can for example reinforce the pity inspired by an old man who *is drifting away little by little*, whereas it was not very important at the outset. But what is its influence? What is the influence of habits and routine? What is the influence of the progressive acceptance of *fate* or resignation to a situation where one knows that only death will bring change?

What are the limits?

The determination to hang on to the bitter end, which seems to animate most carers in the Community, tends to be expressed by phrases such as *going on until it is no longer **possible*** (and not: *necessary*), and indicates the tendency among carers to have a sense of their limits – but what are they? They seem in the first place to be indissolubly linked with the various circumstances and motivations which led to the decision to care, which have been amply described above. These limits also seem to correspond to something vague in the mind of carers. When the care situation starts, some carers establish definite limits beyond which they will not go - because they do not wish to do so, or because they find themselves incapable of doing so - and yet many of them in all countries go beyond the limits just the same. Reality turns out different from their previous ideas and convictions; their progressive involvement under the influence of a slow process of physical or psychological deterioration on the part of their relative does not make it easy for them to recognise that, as the days go by, their initial limits have been reached or even exceeded. Their experience or the discovery of capacities which they did not believe they possessed, can push back the boundaries. The vagueness of these limits results partly from the development of the carer in relation to the situation experienced. This situation is determined not only by the recipient of care, but also by the other people in the immediate environment, including professional carers.

Limits to caring are often conceived in terms of the onset of senile dementia or incontinence. For descendant carers, the need to provide hygienic assistance, especially to the parent of the opposite sex, is frequently expressed as a barrier to continuing care. The reality of incontinence (especially faecal), dementia, and even more, the appearance of both, although they are often managed by the carer, frequently mark the threshold of breakdown, as shown by the main reasons given for the decision actually taken to place the patient in an institution. Of all care situations, probably the most difficult and intolerable is looking after an elderly person suffering from senile dementia.

Emergency solutions

A first solution consists in seeking (or strengthening) external aid, either informal or formal, and getting out of certain tasks.

I always promised myself that I would not cross the threshold of washing my mother ... her personal hygiene, you know. And the day when she was no longer able to do it herself, I asked for a nursing assistant. It's working out well. (France)

However, things are not always as simple as in the case of that woman: getting assistance presupposes the existence and accessibility of home services, or personal financial resources to pay for professional help. As regards informal aid, this presupposes the existence of siblings or descendants, or possibly neighbours, and their willingness to co-operate. Now, as the British report underlines, "the other members of the family may withdraw once the principal carer has been identified". The available data do not allow us to evaluate the frequency of this type of behaviour, nor the rate of success of carers who try to make them change their minds. Solidarity and mutual help between siblings can also be found, but here again the data are inadequate to undertake a comparative analysis between Member States.

A second solution consists in *passing on the torch*: several national reports mention this, but it appears that it is not very frequent and tends to be reserved for cases where the carer gives up or is not in a fit state to continue. A solution which tends rather to come from the four southern countries, but which also applies, although less frequently as one moves north, consists in sharing roles and functions, and this solution may be set up from the beginning of a caring process.

[] Responsibility *rotates* between different carers, and the recipient of care does not move; or

[] The recipient of care *rotates* between the homes of his or her children (even if they are far away).

In these two cases, there is no fixed carer.

[] Brothers and sisters share the tasks and functions equitably, although one of them is the principal carer.

A third solution consists in deciding to place the patient in an institution. Leaving aside any objective reason why this cannot be done (absence of residential facilities or excessive financial cost, for example), this solution appears to be affected by a solid taboo: in all Member States carers agree explicitly that they only see this possibility as an extreme solution. It is however possible that spouses providing care have less difficulty in deciding this, because (or on condition that) they enter the institution together.

The burden which a number of carers, wherever they live, agree to bear beyond their limits, suggests that they still prefer to *drain the chalice to the dregs* rather than adopt this solution.

4. The effects of time

The everyday dimension

The report on the United Kingdom points out that the everyday life of the carer is mostly a function of three criteria:

[] the type and degree of dependence of the patient,and the needs for care deriving from this;

[] the extent of the personal involvement of the carer;

[] the type of household and the possible presence within the household of other people besides the carer and the dependent relative.

As the care provided varies between total care of an invalid confined to bed requiring a round-the-clock presence, or a sporadic type of care here and there, there is no one typical day (but there are certainly types of day according to the criteria mentioned above).

The French report deals with the importance of routine, which on the one hand is necessary for efficient running and is reassuring, but on the other hand is tiring. It points out that the absence of routine resulting for example from the patients instability, which can go so far as to disrupt the running of the household in cases of grave mental deterioration, is a factor which destroys the normal rhythm of everyday life.

> It's incredible the number of silly tricks she gets up to ...
> I get her dressed, then I leave her for just a moment and when
> I get back she has taken off everything and put her knickers
> on her head. She has a mania for tidying ... in a manner of
> speaking because she moves the forks into the sewing-box, lays
> out the dirty linen in the wardrobes, throws things out, ...
> you'd have to live through it to believe it! How can I
> possibly cope with this to have a clean house and a meal on
> the table when everybody is hungry? Everything gets on top of
> me ... I'm going to end up crazy like her. (France)

German research has produced similar findings: a variable alternation between routine and changes, as a function of day-to-day needs or the sudden destruction of all organisation by an unexpected event, uncertainty due to the fact that one does not know whether a change is transitory or definitive - all these factors with a decisive effect on daily life, demanding considerable flexibility from the carer [Braun, 1991].

The evolving care situation

Seventy per cent of carers questioned in a survey in Ireland do not think that the situation is going to get better. Although the other countries do not have figures which can be compared to the Irish ones, all national reports which deal with the question of the evolving situation express an exclusively negative view of it, because once it has started, the dependence of an elderly person generally gets worse, either in a slow process or by degrees.

Given the shortage of research in this area, mentioned by most reports, the following observations on changes which have taken place are based more on the six qualitative studies.

The consequences for the carer's health

Although it is often difficult to know whether a deterioration in health, or an illness, results from the caring situation, one can state from the outset that such a situation seldom has a positive impact on health.

A second fact appears certain from the existing research: given their age, **spouses** providing care are more exposed to health problems than descendants providing care. Having become more fragile, they have less resistance, and if they are involved in care which stretches them beyond their strength (notably their physical strength), the situation exposes them to major risks to their own health. In addition, they are frequently unable to rest as often as their condition would require, and to preserve their health.

This same phenomenon of not being able to take care of one's own health, or to keep in shape, on account of a lack of time as well as weariness about *one more thing to be done*, is equally true of descendants providing care, which in a certain sense marks them as potential care-receivers of the future.

A third phenomenon is the strong tendency of carers, whether spouses or children, to experience psychosomatic reactions.

> *I have stomach pains; it seems that they are coming from the care situation, which makes me very tired. (Germany)*

> *I have had a very serious intestinal illness, which clearly reflects how tense the situation is. (Germany)*

Overwork, general fatigue, back pain, physical and mental exhaustion, weakening of strength and resistance, nervousness, irritability, anxiety, insomnia, a state of depression, etc. - these are the faithful companions of carers from Greece to Ireland, from Italy to Portugal, from Spain to Germany. However, of course, not everyone exhibits deterioration in their health; the extent of change is not documented systematically in existing research.

Changes in relationships due to the care situation

These changes touch several aspects of social life: the relationship between the carer and the dependent person, the marital relationships of the carer and with the children for whom he or she may still have responsibility, relationships between siblings, relationships outside the family.

A reading of the national reports imposes a preliminary observation: it seldom happens that a care situation, in one way or another, does not affect one's whole network of relationships; only rural society in Spain (or at least Catalonia) seems to stand as an exception to this rule, because of its concept of care.

Leopold Rosenmayr points out that "our society lacks the capacity (...) to recognise the need for verbal exchanges between individuals. Communication is not considered as something vital, but as something which one does casually" [Rosenmayr, 1988: 9]. The French semi-directive interviews, in particular, show how the carers fail to discuss problems with the dependent person, their husband, their sisters or their brothers; but then they resent them for being unaware of the difficulties of the situation. Thus, negotiation between the different parties involved, precisely on the carer's limits and needs, is rare. The absence of communication, the carer's inability to be clear, and the carer's silence, make the situation more oppressive and lead to conflicts. The practice of keeping quiet can go very far:

A married woman took care of her mother, who was physically incapacitated but living on her own, and regularly organised the temporary reception of her mother in a geriatric institution so that she could go on her holidays. Under pressure of marital conflict generated by the care which she was providing, she resigned herself to put her mother permanently in the institution. She took this decision on her own. Six months later, her mother was still unaware of the definitive nature of her stay, and that she had no home to go to any more. Even the (comprehensive) insistence of the geriatrician in the institution was of no avail: the daughter did not dare to reveal the true position to her mother. The price of silence was high: marital relations deteriorated because she resented her husband; the elderly mother was sad and *disorientated*, and began to suffer from a loss of mental health; the daughter herself suffered from depression.

The relationship between the carer and the recipient of care (see above) is nourished both by the shared experience of the two (childhood or married life) and by the history of the individual. The emotional burden means that it cannot be unchangeable, and can lead to rapid and frequent switches between positive and negative reactions.

> *I slapped my father once - I couldn't take it any more, he was driving me mad. Afterwards I could do nothing but cry, cry ... with shame. The worst was when he took my hand to say that he understood. (France)*

It is easily imagined that the relationship between the carer and their dependent relative is an extremely complex and diverse one.

A number of carers who were questioned (German, French, Greek, Dutch) stress the **positive** evolution of the relationship with their parent for whom they are caring. Three types emerge:

[]   The (re)discovery of old reciprocal bonds of affection.

[]   The construction of a new adult relationship on the basis of the recognition of each person's identity and the creation of strong bonds of affection; **such a construction implies dialogue.**

[]   The maturing of the carer through an inner process.
     Example of a son: *I've changed. In the beginning I just saw it as a terrible chore, but for the last three or four years... Today I am devastated to see her getting so weak. I started loving her and pitying her. I always said that I wouldn't get involved, but then something was awakened inside me. At the beginning I took her as a burden ... not any more. Now I think "poor old thing"(...). When I take her temperature, I don't do it as a duty to be got through. I have learned to love her while taking care of her. (Greece)*

The relationship between parents (one of whom is the caring spouse) and children seems everywhere to be dominated by reactions of solidarity between descendants; the six qualitative studies bring this out. Some parents consult their children on the decisions to be taken or the solutions and types of aid to be applied; here again, there is dialogue.

Could one conclude that as long as one of the parents carries out the role of principal carer, and thereby gives the children only the role of assistant carers, siblings find it easier to feel solidarity? We do not have the information to examine all possible developments in this field of relationships once the patients health gets worse or the caring parent becomes equally dependent.

The marital relationship of the (descendant) carer seems inevitably affected, because the spouse cannot really remain neutral. The data do not allow one to conclude whether positive or negative developments predominate, although there are many cases of marital conflict arising from a decision to provide care; these can be read in most of the national reports. Those reports seem to identify the fairly generalised tendency in cases of marital conflict that it is the man - i.e. the carer's husband - who plays *the killjoy*, and the reverse rarely happens. There are though some reservations about the objectivity of the reporting, because the whole history of the couple is involved, and besides, in the interviews, only the carer was speaking[1].

---

1   Example of a (French) married woman, living with her husband and their twenty-year-old daughter, still at home. After her father had an accident, they took her parents in; the father is bedridden, incontinent and blind, the mother alcoholic and senile. The principal feature of the relationships between one side and the other is rivalry, with the carer as the target. Undoubtedly, the husband shows more hostility than understanding and support; but one would have to mention that the old sick parents are occupying the couple's bedroom, and the couple have been sleeping for the last three years on the sofa in the living-room, and have thus given up intimate relations.

Restrictions on free time

These restrictions and their repercussions on social and leisure activities, or indeed on the carer setting out on holidays, are widely reported in the national reports. Not surprisingly, social restrictions seem to be related most of all to:

[]   the type and degree of dependence;

[]   the type and volume of care received;

[]   organisational abilities;

[]   the pressure of effective needs for time and activities for oneself.

This list seems applicable to all countries. Variations appear to depend on situations and carer's attitudes.

[]   Carers who know how to get help and are able to do so do not suffer any restrictions – or few – in their relationships, their leisure activities and their holiday arrangements. The *French typology* brings out the fact that neither the type nor the degree of dependence are decisive; rather, it is the *underlying* attitude of the carer (except in cases of heavy dependence compounded by absence of assistance): this type of carer knows – and reacts in keeping with this – that the quality of care and the quality of his or her own life as a carer are dependent on maintaining a personal balance, and that this can be done by preserving as far as possible one's own life, claiming certain rights and **planning** to have some time off.

[]   The *counter-example*, according to the French analysis, is provided by carers practising *total immersion* in the care situation: their caring role is confused with their *raison d' tre*, they identify their needs with those of the dependent relative, and abandon their own personality. This model of reaction seems to be set in the old relationship between the carer and the recipient of care; the carer suffers an effective loss of external relationships, leisure activities and holidays. But this reduction is not really justified by the objective situation: the relative could remain alone, or there is an offer of assistance, or the dependent person is more autonomous than the carer wants to admit.

[] Restrictions on free time, and the corollaries of this, are real for most carers; this is the case particularly where there is a combination or a build-up of several features: absence or low level of external assistance, intense need for care and/or supervision, work activities, financial difficulties, weariness, loss of energy or isolated dwelling.

The Greek and Spanish reports identify different difficulties according to the sex of the carer: life and leisure activities of women are concentrated on three main areas: home, family and Church; thus, the fact of being more confined to the home has a lesser effect on their activities and contacts apart from those connected with the Church. For men, the centres of attraction are *outside the walls*: the café and the *town square*; they are thus affected more strongly by restrictions and privations when care for their relative keeps them at home.

Practical changes

These changes are numerous and diversified, and have a very varied impact on individuals or the family group. What follows is simply a non-exhaustive listing, considering that it needs no comment:

[] moving into co-residence with the recipient of care;

[] modifications to the home
Examples:
Installing a child's bed in the bathroom to free a room for the bedridden father - Setting up the bedridden patient in the living-room so as to integrate her or him into family life - Moving house to the older person's home, because the house is

bigger; adding a toilet or shower near to the dependent person's bedroom.

[] deprivation or even financial impoverishment;

[] improvement in material conditions
Example:
The carer with no financial resources (divorce, widowhood, unemployment, etc.) benefits from shelter and the pension income of the person being cared for;

[] confinement to the home.

5. Carers in paid employment

As women are largely predominant among descendant carers, their rising rate of occupational activity often leads to the conclusion that the potential contribution of family carers will decline. This conclusion is apparently corroborated in Denmark which has the highest level of female employment and the lowest level of family care in the European Community.

Less hasty analyses and conclusions take account of the State-based concept of care for elderly dependent people (the Danish State takes responsibility for this) and the widespread availability of caring services in the home. One therefore realises that the cause- and-effect linkage may be the other way around: **because** women are liberated from the obligations of a demanding care situation, they are free to work.

The Dutch situation seems rather to prove the weak link of cause and effect between paid work and the caring role; the Netherlands are distinguished in the Community by the lowest level of female employment, but despite this, family care for the dependent elderly does not seem to be higher than elsewhere.

Other contributing factors are the work timetable, the number of hours of absence from the home (full-time or part-time working; commuting time) or again the tiredness caused by working.

It appears obvious from the different reports that the combination of work and a caring role is rarely easy, that it is restrictive, and that it needs a high degree of organisation especially when the state of dependency is a heavy one.

Stress and the competition between the two activities, a feeling of doing both jobs badly, and a feeling of guilt seem to be frequent occurrences.

> *When I'm at home looking after my mother, my mind is in the office. When I'm at work, I'm worrying about what may be going on at home. (France)*

> *I forget everything. I go to work and I've forgotten to shave. (Greece)*

Solutions adopted

The best response seems to be to delegate a maximum number of tasks to other people, whether paid or unpaid, on whom one can depend. Some people go so far as to employ a daily minder on a paid basis all day. The solution of placing the elderly parent in a residential institution appears to be rejected by the working carers as often as the others (but only those who have remained carers were questioned). Having regard to the negative attitudes towards institutions, it seems likely that several reasons are needed to give priority to occupational activity at the expense of the provision of care.

The adoption of part-time working seems fairly common in all countries, but is generally connected with *female experiences*. This solution, which makes it possible to reconcile the two areas, does not contain as many drawbacks as a total cessation of work activity; although terms and conditions of part-time employment may be relatively disadvantageous.

Home working is a solution which is still rather rare, but is felt to be beneficial by those who practise it, especially when they are co-resident with the recipient of care.

6. The *burden* of caring

Financial problems and repercussions on the carer's health obviously weigh heavily on the care situation; these problems have already been dealt with, and will not be restated in the present chapter.

Generally speaking, it is the sum of **a whole set of difficulties** which makes the situations so burdensome. As time goes on the burden increases for most; the duration is indeterminate and almost always lengthy.

Analysis of national reports has not brought out significant differences between Member States or *categories* of countries. Thus, each of the quotations from carers which are dotted through the text which follows could come from any one of the different countries.

The sociological analysis of the carer in rural Spanish society indicates that the burden to be borne varies according to *categories of families*: when the family network is close-knit and there is strong cohesion and solidarity within the group, the carer's lot is made more bearable, even in the absence of practical assistance. The qualitative studies from other countries corroborate this finding, especially the ones from Greece and France, which point out that it is not exclusive to rural societies but because it is found there in *purer* form it is more visible. Moreover, the structure and context of rural society seem more favourable to the cohesion of the family group than its geographical fragmentation in an urban setting.

Significantly, it appears that the burden of caring is differently experienced depending on whether the carer is a descendant or a spouse of the recipient of care. This hypothesis merits wider analysis and discussion to disentangle factors such as co-residence and sex of the carer.

Emotional, psychological and social problems

Caring for a dependent older person - unlike caring for children or young invalids - is not in itself a *project for life*: rather the usual way out is the death of the dependent relative.

One carer said: "it is the ungrateful task of a Cinderella who will not be set free by a Prince Charming in a fine carriage, but by a hearse which will carry away the object of all her cares." [Lépine, Nobecourt, 1988].

This fundamental fact, oppressive in itself, may lead the carer in a crisis situation to desire the death of the person being cared for. Such a desire sets off other difficult psychological phenomena: it creates a terrible sense of guilt, and as it cannot be admitted it cannot be stated in words by the carer. (Hence the benign influence of support groups, where this is stated openly and is listened to without value judgements.)

The sense of guilt can have other reasons: the idea of not doing enough, or not doing it well enough, the fact that one has got carried away, that one has used violent words or gestures, the sensation that one has abandoned the patient, because one has claimed some freedom or some fun by going to the cinema or going on holidays.

The fact of watching day by day the slow deterioration or the suffering of the patient is difficult; it provokes feelings in the carer such as tenderness, compassion, sadness or powerlessness. It generates an anguish of death, anguish about one's own death and the death of the other person. It provokes the *mirror effect*: the caring spouse sees his or her own reflection, the younger carer sees his or her possible future, and sees what old age may be. This leads to questioning about the continuity of care if the carer happened to die before the patient, or if the carer fell ill, becoming dependent in turn and unable to carry on. This question is all the more worrying when the carer is old herself, or if although younger he or she is aware of having a serious illness.[1]

A sentiment which runs counter to the **desire** for death is the **fear** of it. This fear of losing one's father or one's mother (in the cases observed, in Greece and France) is linked to existential questions concerning the carer - *what am I going to become without her/without him*? - these questions could arise for example in a very symbiotic son/mother relationship, or where there is financial dependence on the patient's pension. Fear of the other person's death can also be felt between elderly spouses, after a long history of marriage.

> *I just want one thing: that we could stay together for a long time still. My wife has had her two legs amputated, she is almost blind, but she is not suffering. (France)*

The care situation and the burden which it imposes frequently generate stress, frustration, nervousness, irritability, disquiet, anxiety, or constant worry in the carer. These sensations and reactions work against the enormous patience (stressful in itself) which the carer has to show, often without interruption, and not only if the dependent older person suffers memory loss.

Even when, objectively speaking, the care being provided is not very substantial in itself, the consequences for the carer's psychological state can be considerable. All the national reports record the mental

---

1   One of the women questioned for the French qualitative study, is helping her mother who is still relatively healthy but is very elderly and lives on her own. She persuaded her mother to go into sheltered housing. This woman carer knows that she has a serious illness; she also knows that her husband will not carry on where she leaves off; they have no children. The carer's elderly mother and her husband do not know about her illness, and they do not know that this is a preventive move.

fatigue of carers, their exhaustion because they are psychologically at the end of their tether.

> *I am worn out, physically and morally. I am so tired. (...) Sometimes I say, "My God, give me peace ... I can't go on, I can't go on any further. Why do I have to die myself?" That's the sort of condition I'm in (Greece).*

A number of difficulties arise from the relationship between the carer and their relative. The provision of care for elderly parents, according to the French report, includes "a multitude of situations; the heterogeneous nature of these situations ranges as widely as might be expected from the personal reactions of any two adults, shaped by their own personality, their personal history and a shared past which is differently experienced by each person. (...) It would appear that in these diversified emotional experiences, *negative* feelings prevail over *positive* feelings."

Among the difficulties emphasised in the national reports, a prominent feature is the character of each person - or rather the character of the recipient of care.

> *I get no pleasure from living with my mother; it makes me depressed. The eight years that I have spent looking after her have really wrecked me, because she is not only selfish, but incredibly pessimistic. (Spain)*

Apart from long-established character traits, what is difficult to put up with are changes in character, under the effects of age, suffering and dependence. When the elderly person finds it difficult to accept and live through the state of dependence, and, even more significantly, deterioration, he or she may become sad, depressive, introverted, bitter, grumpy and aggressive. These reactions, which are an expression of suffering, inevitably overflow onto the carer.

A quite different aspect of the carer/relative relationship is the inversion of roles, which is brought out in all the national reports, but is generally not fully analysed in its psychological complexity andsignificance for the carer. The two *traditional* forms are on the one hand, an inversion of the daughter/mother relationship, and on the other hand the inversion that takes place between spouses.

> *She just asks for something to eat. I feed her prawns, a piece of chocolate. She is like a baby ... how can I explain? (Greece)*

The content analyses of the semi-directive interviews carried out for the French qualitative study have identified some distinctive phenomena among the reactions of descendants and spouses, the reactions of carers and dependent older relatives, the reactions of men and women.

> "Where children are concerned (...), the difficulties are found more among the daughters than the mothers: their problems show a non-acceptance of the changed personality of their mother, or the need for the support of a mother when faced with psychological suffering. The difficulties experienced by sons seem more particularly connected with the fact that a mothering instinct is probably not innate in men. (...)

The inversions of roles between spouses appear less complex, and in the cases under observation they take place apparently without major problems: husbands seem better able to take on a *maternal role* if they are helped by nurses, and if this transfer also brings them back to their masculine role of *prince saviour* (...); women take on the masculine role of authority and decision-making although they had previously worked in a submissive role. For them there is thus a real inversion of roles, whereas for the husbands there is the addition of a role which is allegedly female.

> These observations lead to the following rule: for a role inversion to be carried through without (too much) conflict, its acceptance must be bilateral."

Losses

Losses are mainly connected with the lack of freedom and time (real or experienced as such).

> *Emotionally, you're involved all the time. I can never go out. I always need someone looking after her. It's a rope around my neck: you're never free - and that's difficult to live with. (Netherlands)*

> *He has invaded my life. (Germany)*

> *Your whole life is confined, you can't go out when you want to. Buying clothes for yourself, you only do it if you really need them. But as for living a normal life like everybody else ... that you can't do. When you see other people, you say to yourself: "Oh, what a tough life I'm leading." (Netherlands)*

As emphasised by the Spanish report, "in cases of extreme dependence (...) carers are imprisoned in their roles (...), and their social, family and professional life is severely limited by this. When there is a lesser degree of dependence, carers live in the fear of deterioration on the part of the elderly person, and the impact which this will have on their lives."

This link between the degree of dependence and loss of freedom is further refined by the *French typology*: this shows "that the burden to be borne is not particularly a function of objective factors - as for example the type and degree of dependence or the fact of a combination of functions: occupational activities and care provision in particular - but that it is more bound up with socio-psychological factors such as the type of relationship between the carer and the recipient of care, the personality of the carer, his or her personal history, the type of emotional dimension involved, the cohesion of the family group", the extent to which outside help is used. That is to say, in some ways, the carer's ability and will to restructure his or her time in relation to objective needs of the dependent older person play a considerable role.

The lack of freedom and time creates frustrations, making it impossible to recharge one's batteries, or causing losses of energy and of will to take on anything at all.

The consequences are multiple:

[]   never being *at ease*, not being alone;

[]   elimination of all spontaneity in time use; if the dependent person needs a constant presence, any absence on the part of the carer has to be painstakingly organised in advance;

[]   a reduction, or even abandonment of personal activities, leisure interests, meetings with friends or family, going out, going on trips, taking holidays – and sometimes even of marital relations.

The financial losses, both direct and indirect, have already been mentioned due to the extra costs associated with meeting needs of dependence, due to the reduction or cessation of occupational activity (loss of salary and social insurance).

The weight of dementia

This thing is insufferable (Greece)

Caring for a parent who has declined mentally is widely regarded as the hardest thing of all. In many different situations, this type of illness has a sort of *magnifying effect*; everything is heavier, and the difficulties involved in the provision of care are amplified.

These disorders are generally accompanied by urinal and faecal incontinence (as a consequence of the loss of memory), which tends to add considerably to the tasks and their burdens.

According to the different national reports, four specific phenomena generate the peculiar burden of these care situations:

[]   the changed personality of the person with dementia;

[] the loss of memory;

It's very hard to see somebody that you knew in good health and who now doesn't recognise you any more (...) You grit your teeth, you look at this stupid (...), dirty person ... and you flip. If your daughter happens to say something to you, then you are ready to snap... All you can do is grit your teeth... It's hard (...) I have become very different from what I was, I get cross very easily. (Greece)

[] the destruction of the relationship;

[] the impossibility of any verbal communication.

The consequences are of a practical and a psychological kind.

The practical consequences which make daily life more difficult and harassing are, for example, the major unpredictability of any day and the need for flexibility in any organisation, the absence of routine, the continual need for supervision, the risk of running away, the management of anomalies and dysfunctions, and the extent of extra domestic chores.

Everything suggests that the psychological repercussions are more extensive than the practical ones, large though they are. Even if the elderly person is only mildly affected – that is to say, they **only** have memory problems – it is extremely tiring for the carer to listen endlessly to the same stories, the same questions, and to be endlessly forced to repeat the same remarks, observations and responses.

I sometimes shout: "But I've already told you a thousand times!" That really sets my nerves on edge. It's stupid to shout... I know perfectly well that she doesn't do it on purpose, but she doesn't know any more, I get ashamed. (France)

Other things which are hard to accept are, in particular: the erasure of shared history; the fear that the illness may be hereditary; the feeling of shame in relation to other people; helplessness when faced with crises of agitation or upset on the part of the elderly person; the never-ending fear of what may happen; the disappearance of affection for the person being cared for; to be replaced by bitterness; the nagging worries about one's stamina to carry on; and the *shameful* idea that there is nothing left but a residential home.

There is a great deal of silence surrounding the work of carers.

7. Care for carers

> *I think that when you look after somebody in your own home, they should say: "Here is what you need" (Netherlands)*

The decision in the research reports to give prominence to more difficult care situations underlines the heavy weight of the burden borne by many carers. It is undoubtedly true for all countries in the European Community that carers in general have a great need for support - practical, material, emotional and social.

As formal assistance has been mentioned in the first part of the report, this section concentrates on informal supports.

Informal help

The importance of the social integration of the carer and his or her membership of social networks emerges clearly in the national reports. As reflected in the German report: "Taking a general view, it appears clearly that the existence of solid social networks around the carer has a major liberating effect, although the carer is still bearing the main burden." Networks, both formal and informal, which support the work of the principal carer are experienced as essential in continuing to look after the dependent person despite all difficulties; they are essential because they prevent the carer from being immersed gradually in greater and greater isolation.

Family setting

Sons and daughters generally show solidarity towards their parents when one of these older persons is performing a caring role (or when both parents are helping each other as best they can).

When **the principal carer is a descendant**, the situation is less clear and various scenarios can co-exist. In bare outline, they may be divided into two contrasting types: solidarity from siblings towards the one of them who has taken on the principal role, or else their disengagement (although they may not necessarily act all together). The former attitude appears to predominate, although it rarely manifests itself in an equitable sharing of tasks, decision-making power or even financial costs; the second type of reaction appears to be more readily adopted when the principal carer is a sister.

> ... and then I ask myself why I always have to be muggins.
> (Netherlands)

> One of my sisters, I never see at all. She says that she is very caught up in her work and that her husband is very demanding and that her children take up a lot of time. In her eyes I don't exist and all I had to do was act like her: not to take in my mother. With the others, it's different. They help me a lot and pay attention to me. (France)

> We are three sisters and we organise everything together. My mother lives with my eldest sister because she has the biggest house. When she goes out to work in the morning, I arrive and I look after everything until she gets back. She provides security at night and I provide work during the daytime. The third sister lives a little further away; she mostly looks after the weekend. Mummy likes going to their place, and that leaves us free. For holidays, we organise it in the same way, each taking turns. (France)

Leaving aside the impact on other people of the attitudes and behaviours that the principal carer adopts in relation to them, combinations of carer and assistant carers are determined by the circumstances and choices (explicit or implicit) which identified the principal carer or led him or her to volunteer (geographical closeness and more particularly, long-standing co-residence, housing conditions, absence of paid employment.

A number of reports, tending to derive more perhaps from the northern countries of the Community, show how siblings tend to stand aside from the tasks and concerns of everyday life - possibly quite happy that the main burden is spared them. Many of them place their confidence in the principal carer; others may give in easily to the option of depending completely on the principal carer; they may even tell themselves that after all their sister decided on this herself. It is equally true on the other hand that the principal carer for a variety of reasons may wish to act like a *lone ranger*. Consciously or otherwise, the carer may reserve an exclusive position of caring, adopting a protective attitude with regard to the others (considering oneself better placed or less overworked in other ways). The carer may find comfort in the situation of a victim, may underestimate the willingness of people to help, and may make the mistake of failing to communicate the need for help to other people.

Whatever the attitudes and behaviours of siblings connected with the two main types of reaction (solidarity or withdrawal), an absence of conflict is rare. Among other things, the solidarity and balance of bonds between the siblings determine whether and how these conflicts are tackled and resolved.

This complex domain of relationships and interactions between siblings appears to be as yet insufficiently explored in the reports on care. In particular, the influence of money as a destructive - or on the other hand a bonding - factor rarely seems to have been examined.

Help received from the family circle
It emerges from existing research that the majority of carers are not abandoned to their fate but indeed receive help and moral support from their family circle, which often forms a sort of *lifebelt* around them.

[] Mutual financial assistance is not exceptional, perhaps most particularly in highly disadvantaged economic settings, to help subsidise the basic needs of the carer and the person being cared for, but it can also happen that a brother or sister *with money* simply pays in order to be completely exempt from other responsibilities. In Greece, the members of a family living together "normally combine their resources which in most of the cases (of those interviewed) come down to pensions. This strategy is normal in Greek society because the family tries to *maximise* its income; the members adopt a survival strategy as a group, rather than acting as economically independent individuals."

[] Solidarity between siblings often leads to sharing, for example the distribution between them of various tasks and time periods: it is probable that this is more frequent when the carer and the elderly person are not co-resident. Another method of sharing consists in total assumption of responsibility on a transitory (but regular) basis, on a fixed day every week, during weekends, or for several weeks in a row.

[] The most frequent configuration seems to be where the principal carer looks after everyday tasks and responsibilities - which generally means the hardest part - and the supplementary carers (spouse, brothers, sisters, etc.) look after the *social contribution* (visits, walks, conversations, transport, taking the patient to the doctor, to the bank), administrative tasks, minor items (small household repairs, for example) or shopping.

As regards the social contribution, this was emphasised in reports from southern countries: the Spanish, Greek, Italian and Portuguese reports emphasise the older person's need for social integration, especially if confined to the house by reduced mobility; the carer then attaches special importance to the family circle satisfying these needs. It should be remembered that in the southern countries - with the possible exception of large cities - *the family circle* embraces all family relationships.

My sister-in-law does not come often, but when she comes my mother is always delighted because she likes her voice and her kindly manner ... although that isn't much help to me. (Greece)

Carers in the more northerly countries may be more negative about these social contributions. They may feel bitter thinking that the others are taking on the easy and agreeable tasks, *playing the good parts*, and leaving them the unpleasant work; so they question the value of this type of intervention, and consider that it is not really any help.

Really helping? ... no. They come around regularly, all right, but not to help. (Netherlands)

Simple visits are experienced more positively by carers who know how to benefit from them and take time for them.

[]   The emotional support of the carer by family members is generally emphasised, whether one is dealing with spouses or children providing care.

With my husband and mother-in-law I can speak with an open heart. (Germany)

I've got my daughter ... but I can't tell her everything, otherwise there are two of us crying. (Germany)

Sometimes I shout, I roar, I've had more than I can bear ... luckily they're there, to understand, to know, to hear me. Without them, I couldn't manage. (France)

The acceptance of the situation by the family circle is obviously of special importance to the carer, as it provides security. If the husband or the young children disapprove of the wife or mother taking care of their relative and create internal rivalries, the conflict-laden atmosphere merely increases the burden of the carers situation.

One may mention the case of a family - husband, wife, adolescent child - who took in the wife's mother. In order to avoid open conflict, the wife (the carer) strictly forbade her mother to show her face in the house as long as her husband was in: the old lady was therefore locked up in her room every evening and at weekends. Any failure to respect this rule on the part of the mother - who grew more and more impatient with being treated inconsiderately, and started to make surprise appearances during family meals - was a source of violent emotion on the part of her daughter, who projected onto her mother the conflict which she was experiencing with her husband. (France)

Obviously, not all carers are in the happy position of that Greek woman (who has been looking after her invalid mother for a very long time) who says "luckily I have a good husband" and who hears him replying "my wife is an angel".

The neighbours

The national reports on Member States situated in the north of the European Community reveal a certain consensus as regards the interventions of neighbours. These are generally limited and rarely go beyond practical, detailed and precise tasks: shopping, transport, use of a telephone, visits to the dependent person and/or carer, company, relieving the carer for an hour or two; sometimes (where there is not co-residence), neighbours have a key so that they can get in if needed, while others are in regular telephone contact with the carer.

A characteristic of these situations is the **non-conferral of responsibility on neighbours** (or an extremely limited designation of responsibility). This same type of behaviour is found in the southern countries, but appears rarer, or possibly limited to city dwellers.

The Spanish, Portuguese and Greek reports underline the importance of the role of the neighbours particularly their **social** functions, in favour both of the carer and of the person being cared for. What one has apparently is a strong degree of cohesion, long-established, probably supported by the religious community to which they belong. The villages *deserted* by young people represent a special case (not only in Greece); the old people who have stayed behind are said to show particular solidarity with each other.

> *They are old themselves ... (the whole village) is just a retirement home. (Greece)*

The doctor - the priest/pastor

Here, one is not really dealing with informal contributors, but the aspects discussed lie on the frontier of their professional roles, at least as far as the doctor is concerned.

As stated in the Spanish report, "in the rural world, doctors and priests play an important role by offering advice and moral support for carers". Although it is not widely treated in most of the reports, the importance of these two *professions of trust* certainly operates in an urban milieu too, but perhaps in a different way.

As regards general medical practitioners, they are often subject to criticism (in Germany and in France for example) not merely because of their lack of geriatric training[1], but also because of their inadequate knowledge of gerontology, especially as regards systems for help and support. They are thus blamed for being ineffective in the area of advice because they do not understand the complexity of the care situation, and they are accused of sidestepping the problem by advising that the elderly person should enter a residential home.

Needs for help and support

These needs are great, and nowhere in the Community is there a balance between *supply* and *demand* (even if Denmark is thought to be approaching such a balance in its services). The French situation, offers an example which is applicable to more than one Member State: "The resources offered are far from matching (...) the needs of families and

---

1   All Member States suffer from a striking shortage of **geriatricians** and geriatric training.

their elderly parents. And the pain of watching a family member declining inexorably is almost always accompanied by fruitless searches and logistical acrobatics for the lack of (...) appropriate services." [Lépine, Nobecourt, 1988]

The needs of carers are a function of several factors, variable according to individual situations and particularly variable according to the general context. Those which seem most decisive in their effects are:

[] siting, accessibility, capacity and professionalism of home-based services;

[] type and degree of dependence of the elderly person;

[] the carer's state of health, emotional strength and physical well-being:

I need a woman to wash her. My father and I do everything, the cooking, the household chores, ... My father is on the verge of collapse. The two of us are more affected than my mother. (Greece);

[] economic level;

[] geographic isolation;

[] social isolation;

[] participation (or non-participation) in the labour market;

[] absence/presence of supplementary informal carers;

[] perhaps the sex of the carer;

[] co-residence or not.

As emphasised in the Dutch report (the same is true in France and probably elsewhere), it is not always easy to know the needs of carers.

They find difficulties in formulating them and - particularly when they are unaware of what exists or could exist in the way of supports and services - in imagining them; they have difficulty in imagining that anything at all could be helpful to them.

Nobody can help me ... except his death. That's a horrible thought. (France)

Financial needs

There is relatively little information on the economic situation of carers, but it is clear that caring usually costs the carer money (apart from all the other *costs* which it has). This extra cost can be absorbed without major difficulty in a number of cases, but causes real financial difficulty to carers from less well-off social groups. The Greek report tells of caring situations of extreme poverty: these situations exist in other Community countries, even in *developed* welfare states.

The financial problems are considerable. We barely have enough to eat. The cost of living is high. A chicken costs 1000 drachmas. Milk ... oh, well... Sometimes she wants something ... (Interviewer: do you go without food?) When we have money, we have something to eat, otherwise we don't (Greece).

More particularly, medical and paramedical costs exceed the resources of a large number of carers, at least in Greece and Portugal.

Financial needs exist on various levels:

[] Income/substitution of income
To a large extent the need for financial assistance derives from the low level of pensions and other income.

Another aspect concerns the various allowances which exist in all countries to subsidise the needs caused by dependence. Generally, difficulties with these allowances may be summed up as follows: the amounts are generally inadequate, the conditions of access are too restrictive, the payments may

have a random character and lead to flagrant injustice, the
bureaucratic procedures are often extremely complicated and,
as for example in Germany, involve hacking ones way through a
jungle of legal regulations.

*We all want the family to help. Me, I'm completely in favour,
but things have to work out differently. I have no income.
Even if the government said to me every year: "Here, take 100
florins for all the money that you're saving us"... In fact,
you are not even entitled to a housing allowance because both
of them have some income, one of them an invalidity pension,
the other a retirement pension: two minimum amounts make up a
maximum! (Netherlands).*

[]   Covering medical and paramedical expenses
     doctors' consultations/visits, nursing care, hygiene care,
     physiotherapy, chiropody, etc.

[]   Coverage of hospitalisation

[]   Coverage of medicine and equipment costs
     pads, hospital beds, wheelchairs, crutches, etc.

Here there is a juxtaposition of the needs of carers and those of the
dependent elderly people, and many of these needs would not exist if
the elderly people had a better financial provision for the costs of
illness and dependence. Furthermore, it is clear that when the
dependent person's pension is inadequate, it is the carer who bears the
extra costs, if that is possible. And in more than one Member State
(Germany and France for example) there is a legal obligation to provide
support.

Carers need to establish independent retirement benefits to secure
their future. The carers themselves are not always aware of this, with
the exception of those who are at work and can foresee either the
reduction or the cessation of their employment before they have reached
retirement age.

We spend so many hours caring, and when we are old ourselves,
that will bring us nothing at all on a financial level.
(Germany)

Whereas these specific financial needs are rarely formulated by the
people most concerned, they have nevertheless entered the public and
political debate, at least in most of the Member States situated
towards the north. Analogous needs exist regarding the social coverage
of carers in case of **illness**.

Needs for practical assistance

Home-based nursing and hygienic care - as well as **help with household
tasks** are of primary importance to support family care in all parts of
Europe, whether or not there is co-residence with the elderly person.
Assistance for tasks and actions requiring major physical effort - to
mention only those - is necessary: thus, in the area of hygienic care,
for example, many carers find themselves in difficulties through lack
of physical strength, when it is a question of giving a bath, lifting
the patient, or even changing the sheets.

It's no use my being a man, but at the age of 82, lifting my
wife who weighs 83 kilos, how am I supposed to manage that on
my own? (France)

A third type of aid figures in the first ranks of urgent needs: the
need for **respite care**. To have some time for oneself, time to breathe,
to put oneself back together, free time without constraints. This need
is not concerned exclusively with the requirements of leisure and
relief; it is also a matter of covering periods of illness or
hospitalisation of the carer, who is all the more worried about this
aspect of the problem if his or her own health is failing, or if he or
she is also very elderly.

The need for intermittent breaks covers a number of ranges: respites
for a few hours, for a day or two (weekends for example) and for
several weeks in a row for holidays.

Leaving aside informal respites organised at family level, between
friends or with neighbours (sources which are probably not always

utilised to the full), the formal services are involved here. In practice, this means:

[]   *granny-sitting* services;

[]   day centres
these always raise the problem of transport, and, according to the French experiences, they may aggravate spatial and temporal disorientation. Clearly, one is not dealing with centres for able-bodied people, with a purely recreational purpose, but facilities for taking in people with diminished autonomy and providing certain forms of care and therapy;

[]   temporary residential care;

[]   holiday stays for dependent elderly people
It may be that this formula is preferable to temporary residential care which may cause effects of guilt on the part of the carer, who feels that the elderly person is being *pigeon-holed* in a place where they will be unhappy, so that the carer can set off to have a good time. If on the other hand the patient also sets off on **holidays**, he or she may also experience an enjoyable break.

This formula is particularly helpful to caring spouses, as they find it difficult to imagine going away other than as a couple. Parallel to the care provided for the dependent spouse by the professional staff - including entertainment - these holiday breaks should include programmes (excursions for example) for the healthier people, i.e. the carers.

While the **hospital at home service** may be an excellent scheme for elderly dependent people, it should not be considered as an aid for carers because the tasks and especially the responsibilities and alienation are increased. Traditional hospitalisation provisionally frees the carer from responsibility for care and - despite the worries arising from the reasons for hospitalisation - allows the carer to benefit from some free time.

Needs for technical equipment

Appropriate technical equipment considerably facilitates the carers work. One may mention for example the hospital bed, the commode, the wheelchair, and crutches. The Dutch report makes it clear that there are advantages when this equipment is provided on a rental basis, both because of the uncertainty about the length of use of the equipment, and having regard to its high purchase price.

This same report also emphasises the need for high-quality equipment, properly maintained.

Psycho-social needs

Any care situation exposes the carer to risks of social isolation particularly as the care-recipient's loss of autonomy gradually progresses. Total isolation is not exceptional and, as underlined by the Spanish report, the care situation can be turned into a *sordid process* of mutual loneliness, with the carer and the patient leading an empty and unsatisfactory life.

The psycho-social need most frequently mentioned during the interviews for the qualitative studies was the need to talk about one's difficulties and the sufferings caused by the care situation, the need to be listened to, to be heard, perhaps even to receive some sympathy.

Attending a support group is very rarely mentioned as a need among carers, with the exception of those who belong to such groups. It is more the case that the positive results obtained by this type of assistance underline the needs at this level.

One common, often recognised need derives from the fact that every effort deserves some recompense: the carer who gives and sacrifices a great deal wants some acknowledgement; he or she needs praise and even thanks.

The need for information and advice

While the Spanish carers who were questioned (qualitative study) felt no need for more information, on the grounds that day-to-day practice is the best apprenticeship[1], there was little support for this conviction among their counterparts in other countries.

The lack of information on services, allowances and rights is felt particularly strongly in the beginning, and all the more so when the dependency is caused by a sudden event. For example, in France, and elsewhere information is fragmented, to such an extent that the carer has to invest a great deal of time and make a number of approaches in order to become informed. Adult children, for lack of information, often feel alone, abandoned and discouraged when they have to take decisions on how to provide care in a crisis situation.

The need for *learning* covers two aspects:

> **Practical** teaching to build up skill
> how to lift a person who has fallen on the ground, even if they are heavy, how to sit them up in bed, how to support them while walking, how to wash them, shower them, etc.; how to change the sheets in an occupied bed.

> *I didn't learn how to look after her. The hardest thing is having to change her incontinence pads all the time. I weigh sixty kilos and she weighs eighty, and I have to roll her first one way, then the other, in order to change the pads. This is really tiring - and nobody ever taught it to me: I went through the hardest path. (Greece)*

[] acquisition of **knowledge** about the illnesses, dependency and its course; this need seems most pressing when the patient suffers from mental deterioration.

---

1 Men are however excluded from this on account of their lack of experience in the area of care and domestic chores, and because nothing in their education prepared them for a caring function.

Acceptability of help and support

At first sight, things look simple, the acceptance of support being the logical outcome of a heavy and constricting burden which leads to a need for help. And indeed it is generally found that where assistance is available, it is willingly received. However, things are a great deal more complex - at least where professional helpers are involved - and it appears that part of the difficulties in accepting help derive from the phase before arrival of outside support.

Irene Steiner-Hummel points out from her research that "the decision in favour of professional care for an elderly parent means first of all the end of a process of decision-making and distancing. (...) (The carer) has to recognise the limits of his or her own resources" [Steiner-Hummel, 1988, 203]. Now, it is not easy to face ones own limits, especially after years of devoted care [Braun, 1991].

The arrival of external helpers means that the principal carer has to *give up some territory* and accept (as well as his or her own limits) the intrusion of strangers into their area, dispossessing them of the exclusive intimacy of the patient, part of the decisions, and also part of their power. Now, "psychologically it is very difficult to let somebody into ones territory and to recognise the other person as a co-operator rather than seeing him or her as a competitor. How can one counter the carers feeling (...) of being called into question?" [Rosenmayr, 1988:8]

Given their strong sense of emotional involvement, women probably feel these difficulties more than men. Descendant carers may be affected more than spouses. Acceptability of help may perhaps be because of their advanced age or the marital relationship, which is very different from the child/parent relationship. With spouses, a particular difficulty should be pointed out: a wife does not always accept the personal hygiene of her husband being looked after by a nursing aide - another woman.

The Dutch qualitative study adds detail on the determining factors in acceptance of outside help. The behaviour of the professionals is the first factor: if the outside helper, secure in a sense of skill, behaves as a *conqueror*, this may simply produce rejection; but if the outsider shows understanding about the situation, and behaves respectfully towards the principal carer, a climate of co-operation may be set up.

> *I ask (the nurses) how to do this or how we could do that together. They give me a lot of advice. You can also let out a yell in their presence when things get on top of you. They act as a buffer. (Netherlands)*

Mutual respect for each others roles and tasks, and the work done by each person, thus appears as a necessary precondition for the acceptability of help.

The Dutch studies also brought out a number of reasons which inhibit carers from looking for external help: distrust of professionals because one does not know who *one is going to come up with*, shame, pride, the fear of being invaded in one's personal and intimate domain, one's home, or again the fear of becoming dependent on another person.

Help from family members is generally accepted with ease, except when there are conflicts. But as already mentioned, difficulties in communication and negotiation may prevent the carer from asking for help from brothers or sisters, spouse or children.

8. Positive aspects

A reading of the different reports leads to the observation - which seems to have a general validity - of close link between the positive aspects and the motivation for providing care for one's elderly parent, ancestor or spouse. The balance between the goal sought and the results obtained seems to be of prime importance. The British report puts forward the hypothesis of a difference according to sex as regards motivations; if this difference is confirmed, it seems likely that the *benefits* deriving from the care situation may also be different according to gender.

A second point to be raised in advance is the rather generalised observation that negative aspects are clearly preponderant in the responses of carers[1]. But can one deduce that these experiences actually prevail over the positive aspects? The question remains open; but one cannot overlook the fact that very often the interview (particularly the semi-directive interview) with the carer represents an *opening of the floodgates*; very often, this is the first time that the carer is speaking, able to mention his or her sufferings and difficulties, the feelings of rage, revolt and violence[2], or indeed the first time that the carer is expressly invited to do this. (Hence – here again – the importance and benefits of support groups: the verbalisation of difficulties *makes room* for a search and discovery of positive aspects.)

Financial advantages

Financial rewards are divided into two categories, the first having to do with future advantage, and the second being concerned with immediate advantages.

[] Future advantages
Inheritance is undoubtedly a consideration for some carers. In certain cases, the legacy is subordinated to a clause concerning the *implementation* of care, through a moral

---

1 The Greek qualitative study points out that 50% of carers who were questioned stated that they saw nothing positive in their care situation.

2 It should be noted in passing that a heavy veil (not to say a watertight capsule) surrounds all the forms of violence which certainly arise in care relationships, in families as in institutions.

agreement or in legal form. This form expressly gives priority to the carer among the inheritors. In other cases, the will does not include any clause on care, nor does it concede any privilege to the carer.

There is little indication that the prospect of inheritance meant that the carer would have acted differently without it: inheritance is generally not the only motivation.

[]   Immediate advantages
These generally derive from a conscious exchange, and cover a variety of configurations. This kind of reciprocity is observed when the needs of the elderly relative coincide with those of the carer (financial dependence on the elderly person's pension; the carer is housed and fed free of charge, etc.). These circumstances are not exceptional following a divorce or unemployment, for example, and appear to affect women more than men.

Another type of exchange is quite frequent: the dependent person gives money or other gifts to the carer. In this way, the person being cared for conveys recognition of what he or she is receiving, at the same time as satisfying a need to avoid being relegated to the sole position of a *consumer of care*.

Reciprocity acts as a balancing factor in the relationship, for both sides.

A number of authors in the different Member States underline the conflicts which these transfers may generate among the siblings of carers.

A longitudinal study carried out in Luxembourg from 1985 onwards on exchanges between adult descendants and their elderly parents revealed that particularly in cases of co-residence - which is frequent, reciprocity is rare because the **descendants** gain more advantages from the situation than their parents: they are housed free of charge, the house and the grandchildren are looked after by the elderly parent or parents; both the husband and the wife can carry on their jobs, and as they are freed in part from domestic and educational tasks they gain some free time [Bruckler- Damjanovic, 1991: 80]. However, these studies do not introduce the loss of autonomy on the part of the elderly parent as a variable in the situation.

Non-material benefits

The German report points out that carers generally attribute more importance to non-material benefits, although financial advantages play an undoubted role.

The relationship between the carer and the care-receiver, although it has not been analysed much from the point of view of enrichment, seems to occupy a key position; any enrichment implies a maturing process. Thus for example the case already mentioned (in Greece) of the son who took on an ungrateful task at first, but later discovered a change in himself as his mother's condition grew gradually worse, until today his only feelings for her are pity and filial love. This happens when an old affection is rediscovered. It happens when the care situation leads to the construction of a relationship between two **adults** going beyond the previous child/parent transactions. In the cases reported, this affects children who formerly felt little attachment for their parents and previously maintained only distant and conventional relationships with them. The move to build a new relationship seems to imply a process of settling negative aspects of shared experience which allows forgiveness and leads to a relationship with the tensions removed.

The Dutch, French, German, Greek and Portuguese reports emphasise another type of enrichment which derives from the caring relationship: seeing the dependent person in a happier condition (than previously when he or she was in an institution or living alone at home), or receiving gratitude from that person, or again saving him or her from ending up in an institution.

The positive contributions of caring can also be found in **relationships within the family group**. The crisis situation created by the dependence of an elderly parent may generate a new awareness among siblings that the individual is one link in the network of collective family solidarity; it may also create or revive a cohesiveness among siblings. Especially if there is interaction between them in supporting a dependent parent, they can rediscover each other, as adults, and the fact of sharing a concern and goal of aiding their father and mother can bring them together and consolidate their bonds.

The **inner path** on which the carer may embark through the role of accompanying the elderly parent (or spouse) in moving towards death is experienced as a lesson of (and for) life: this companionship involves facing up to reality daily, as is inevitable with dependence and old age, and it brings the carer face to face with his or her own future, leading to meditation on his or her own ageing and death.

The satisfaction which the carer derives from the changes in himself or herself, caused by the care situation, emerges from a number of other facts and phenomena which the national reports point out (mentioned here without any particular order, as it is impossible to establish a hierarchy): the fact that a caring role fills up one's life and gives it a meaning; pride at discovering capabilities and aptitudes better than one had imagined, to succeed and find solutions to practical problems, to go beyond oneself; the satisfaction of meeting the elderly person's desire to die at home; the satisfaction of the *duty accomplished*: keeping the rules and thereby receiving social approval, but also keeping faith with oneself and the moral rules which one has set; the satisfaction of being useful or indispensable to somebody, being responsible for them.

> *You feel content and happy to take care of one of your own family. That's very positive. You think about it when you're calm. Maybe I'll see it in that way too when she dies. Maybe you lose a bit of your tranquillity or you miss a few opportunities; but you've got the satisfaction of having done what you could (Greece).*

The good and bad times experienced by carers suggest a future question about the potential of family care. The generations of current carers, both children and spouses, show evidence of inner strength in relation to the difficulties of life and its frustrations which perhaps a younger generation, living in societies with a strongly hedonistic orientation, do not share, and they would thus be more vulnerable when faced with difficult situations.

9. Projects - the Future

When the care situation is very burdensome or is felt to be so, **the carer lives only in the present**, with the worry of coping with day-to-day events which leave no room for anything else.

> The words of a woman (questioned in the framework of another study) who looked after her husband suffering from Alzheimer's disease, almost to the end, perfectly illustrates this state of affairs:

> *It is only since his death that I am realising little by little that it was a Calvary, that I was a saint. It was frightful, but I wasn't aware of that. I was walking through a dark tunnel with his death at the end, putting one foot in front of the other without having the slightest idea where I was going. Every night, I went to sleep with the thought "so long as I can stick it again tomorrow", and every morning my first thought was "how am I going to hold out until this evening?" (France)*

The uncertainty of developments is another major factor which makes all planning difficult to say the least.

> *How can you plan ahead when you don't know what next week will bring? (Germany)*

> *It could go on for years yet, it could be over tomorrow ... (Netherlands)*

It is common that all short or medium-term plans are made conditional on the dependent person's state of health - and usually they reckon on that condition worsening. An added uncertainty concerns one's own health in the medium and longer term.

Planning for **later on** is inhibited because of the fact that **the realisation of these plans will be** built **most frequently on the death** of the dependent older person or the deterioration of the care situation if the person receiving care goes into an institution.

In all Member States the **continuation of support for the elderly relative at home** constitutes the main plan, so as to stave off the need for institutional care. However, admission to a residential institution can in fact be a plan for a caring **spouse**; because in this case the couple go together into the residential home, so that there is no connotation of *abandonment*.

Definite plans appear to be extremely rare among carers, whatever country they live in. Plans that exist are usually those that have been put off until a later time (plans to go on long journeys, for example) or which are being abandoned, such as the case of one Greek man, who is divorced and would like to remarry, but who feels that his chances are low because as things stand, it will be a question of marrying *along with him* his heavily dependent mother.

The **future**, seen as after the death of the patient, does not really seem to offer any positive factors other than *liberation*. To judge from what the carers say, it would appear to be envisaged rather from a pessimistic point of view: saddled with a difficult experience of old age, many carers seem to be having painful thoughts about their own old age: will their children do for them what they now do for their own parents or spouses? Would it not be better to hope for death (or bring it about) before arriving at that stage? For others, because the person being cared for will die, the future can offer nothing except sadness and confusion.

All the light will have disappeared from my life. (Portugal)

What is going to become of me without her? (France; Portugal)

Now I am left on my own like a dried-up tree in a forest. The wolves should come down at night to eat me and put an end to everything (a very old man after the death of the brother he had cared for) (Greece).

The small number of responses in the national reports on the subject of the future and plans for later give an impression that experience had taught the carers to be very modest about their expectations and desires. They seem to bear their caring role as though they were subject to a fate which must be borne, in which they consider themselves to be insignificant.

POLICY ASPECTS AND RECOMMENDATIONS : CARING FOR CARERS

1. The general problem for welfare

The awareness of carer's problems is developing during a period marked by large structural modifications in society. It is extremely difficult to predict the outcomes of these changes in the decades ahead, but, paradoxically, it is necessary to develop responses today. The traditional forms of the Welfare State seem to be in a stage of partial decay; it is reaching its limits. The new situation calls for redefinition, restructuring and reorientation. A driving force, in all directions, is far-reaching demographic changes, most notably the ageing of populations, a new development in society which has no precedent in the history of mankind, and nobody knows where it will lead us. There are also fundamental changes in the world of work, as well as in family structure, and the tendencies of societies to values emphasising personal *well-being*. The economic pressure due to the *explosion* of public budgets - worrying though this may be - is only a small component in a range of complex movements and consequences.

Most Member States behave as if they have been taken by surprise by the demographic increase in the older elderly, with its concomitant need to provide care for dependency. This has happened at a time when, paradoxically, almost all Member States were making large scale use of early retirement from the labour market. And yet the ageing process was foreseeable and had been announced by demographic projections.

One of the consequences of this unpreparedness is the huge gap between the supply and the demand as regards care for the dependent elderly: the needs for home-based services and for quality residential care are largely unmet, and this is all the more true for people with limited financial resources.

Inadequate public expenditure on social needs in a number of Member States has led to inadequacies in support once elderly people lose their autonomy. Faced with these gaps, who provides the care? The answer is the family, essentially alone rather than in partnership with the state and voluntary sector. The family adapts to changed circumstances and difficulties; it operates in silence and without complaint, often in conditions of extreme hardship, emotional if not material. Whether a country is anchored in the traditional family model, or it has adopted the model of the so-called modern family, overwhelmingly it is the family that copes where the State is deficient.

This fundamental and essential contribution of family care was demonstrated in the main text. However the family cannot do everything, and may be even less able to do everything in our day as the provision of care can go on for a very long time at high intensity. Lifestyle changes, medical progress and environmental improvement have postponed death but, in doing so those illnesses which cause suffering but which do not *kill the patient* have been prolonged. There has been a dramatic increase in diseases which few people used to contract in earlier times, because they were dead before they could do so - especially senile dementia, which leads to such exhaustion when one provides care, and for which few satisfactory care solutions exist. All of these *extra factors*, extra years, extra diseases, and extraordinary social changes can hardly be taken on by the family on its own, *as an extra*.

2. Main characteristics of current policies - convergences and divergences

1. Generally speaking, social policy for older people in Member States is a policy based on **dependence**. Leaving aside certain exceptions (probably Denmark today, and possibly the United Kingdom tomorrow), this is not *policy for the elderly **and** the family*. The highly marginal position of informal carers in social policies for the elderly is a consequence of the very concept on which they are based.

    In this connection, it is interesting that in Britain, since the beginning of the 1980s, feminist researchers have provided solid arguments to suggest that care for the older elderly is a matter of **relationships** within the **family** and the home, and that it forms part of the **daily household activities** of women [Finch, 1991]. While old age and the family are indissolubly linked in reality, government policies split the two.

2. There is a clear direction in the care policies of all **Member** States: community care is given priority over residential care. There are reasons in common for this preference, which are of an economic kind: controlling the growth in health and social expenditure. The priority given to living at home coincides with the desires of the majority of both the elderly and of their families. But there is a divergence of opinion on the extent to which the responsibilities and the major part of the care are to be borne exclusively by the family.

    The political and economic implications of a policy to provide community care for elderly people living at home for as long as possible, involving both formal and informal assistance, fall into two extreme categories in the Community [Walker, 1991b] :

    [] *the soft form*, which is the most widespread one, tries to meet the need to control costs by developing less expensive forms of care for the elderly than institutionalisation;

    [] *the form based on extreme pessimism* - practised by "those governments which have taken up a position against the Welfare State" [ibid.] - aims at exacting a larger contribution from the family, as well as securing growth in the commercial and voluntary sectors [ibid.].

3. In all Member States, there are three coexisting components in the systems for providing care for the older elderly, each of these components having a variable degree of importance according to the country involved: the family (and other informal networks), the formal home care services, operating with paid or voluntary staff, and the residential care institutions. Despite the obvious overlaps between these actors, concerted interaction is rare; their mutual independence frequently leads to inconsistencies, malfunctions and, last but not least, to high costs.

4. In all Member States with the exception of Ireland, there is a distinction between the social and health components of home-based services; this is often true (as notably in France) of residential institutions also. What one finds in France is also applicable to other countries: "fragmented care arrangements (...) tend to subdivide the individual (...) into a number of needs (health care, socialisation, assistance with housework) and each of these needs will be met by a different professional with responsibility for the living conditions of the elderly person." [Guillemard, Pitaud, 1991:77]

In keeping with the aims of this international comparison, which involves providing opportunities to gain from the positive and negative experiences of other countries, it is noteworthy that the plan for the beginnings of a social policy for the elderly, being drafted by the Greek government, involves the application of this same dichotomy.

One may also mention Italy in this connection, as a number of highly diverse innovations, created independently on a one-off basis, are proliferating in that country with a degree of inconsistency, given the lack of co-ordination between the different sectors [Facchini, 1991].

Another very practical example is the *hospital at home* in France: often the local association has a team which includes home helps, and they go into action even if the elderly person already has a home help - i.e. the usual home help is replaced for the duration of the *hospital at home*.

5. Co-ordination - it follows - is thus generally a major missing element factor in the systems which operate in Europe, and this is true on two levels: firstly at the level of the different formal home services between themselves, as well as between those services and the other actors (hospitals, institutions, voluntary associations, the family, etc.). Too often, the different agencies involved see each other (or treat each other) as competitors, thus running the risk of turning the elderly person into their *object* of

care. Secondly, it happens at the level of care provided **around** the dependent person - i.e. based on the needs of both the elderly person and of the carer.

Clearly, once there is negotiation between the formal and informal *partners*, and negotiation over *who* does *what*, co-ordination between the different services should follow in practice.

6. The central role of the family in the provision of care when a spouse or parent has lost his autonomy tends to be known and recognised today in the countries of the Community (although this has involved a process of *rediscovery* for many of them).

But another similarity is the generally theoretical nature of this recognition of the central role of the family. Apart from perhaps the United Kingdom in recent times (see below), no Member State has adopted an explicit policy of support for carers, although a variety of support initiatives can be found in nearly every Member State.

7. Having regard to the social protection offered by a Welfare State in various areas, the expectations of citizens have changed today (if mainly in the northerly countries), in the sense that the various social services and programmes are seen increasingly as a **right.** At the same time, their non-religious character has removed these welfare services from the domain of charity for the least well-off. Thus there is a growing tendency to accept assistance, both on the part of the elderly person and on the part of the family carer.

3. Policies on caring for carers - between utopia and the first practical implementations

Caring for carers, either now or in the future, largely depends on the provision and development of services for community care for elderly people.

This reflects the fact that the same services work to a considerable extent both for the elderly people and for the carers (as for example the two traditional services, help with housework and home-based nursing, but the same applies to services such as alarm systems and meals on wheels). It derives also from the *living alone clause*, explicit or implicit, which in practice conditions the provision of services in a number of Member States: if there is a shortage of places, a selection is made according to the following scale: first to be served are elderly people living alone with no possibility of family aid; followed by elderly couples finding themselves in the same circumstances; and finally lower down the ladder, the carers, both collateral and descendant, with caring spouses in the middle category.

Community care services are either underdeveloped or overstretched, and never manage to meet the needs. To what extent is it realistic, then, to plan (or even hope) that policies for **carers** could be implemented?

[] **Countries more or less characterised by an under-developed range of community care services:** Greece, Ireland, Italy, Portugal, Spain.

It seems utopian to hope that care for carers could emerge (or be developed) as long as the services even for elderly people living alone are barely in existence.

However, **Ireland** may avoid this rather unpromising future: there is a government plan to provide care for carers (although this has not yet been given much substance on the ground).

The recent social policy programme for the elderly - "The Years Ahead" - confirms the pre-eminence of community care and sees public and family assistance to the dependent elderly as complementary supports, although this plan merely reiterates the objectives and recommendations of the 1968 programme (very advanced at that time) which could only be implemented to a minor degree [O'Shea, 1991: 23,24].

- Ireland is the first Member State to follow the British example of assigning an allowance to carers; the allowance comes in for criticism on account of its small amount, and its excessively restricted payment criteria, but it exists.

- In addition, the situation of carers has a sufficiently high profile for widespread discussion, and creation, of a Carers' Charter (Annex 4).

There are, then, several indicators that a policy for family carers in Ireland is being set up. In some respects Ireland can be disassociated from this first group of countries, although its community care policy is limited: from the point of view of caring for carers, this country is not showing the same degree of tardiness.

[] **Countries with a number of home-based services, but which are overstretched:** Belgium, Denmark[1], France, Germany, Luxembourg, Netherlands, United Kingdom.

- The United Kingdom which has - with the Netherlands - the best gerontologic infrastructure in the Community [Walker, 1991b], is also the first Member State to have worked out a policy in favour of carers, alongside a new policy for community care which will increase the emphasis on the private sector and the responsibilities of local government; these policies are described in the White Paper[2] [Cox, 1991:12].

---

1   In Denmark about one-third of services work 24 hours a day, 7 days a week; that the permanent beneficiaries of services represent (1989) 35% of those aged between 75 and 84, and 63% of those aged 85 or over [Plovsing, 1991:9].

2   The White Paper is based on two documents: Caring for People: Community Care in the next Decade and Beyond (1989) and the National Health Service and Community Act of 1990, the first phase of which came into force in April 1991 [Cox, 1991:12].

It was in Britain too that the first National Carers' Association was established[1] (leaflets from one of the local associations are attached to the present text: see annex 5).

It may therefore be considered that **the United Kingdom is the leader in the Community** as regards supportive policy for carers (although because the issue is on the public agenda, carers in the UK may hardly credit this).

. None of the other Member States in this group of countries has so far developed a policy of caring for carers. However, the economic costs of dependence are such that the threat that carers might desert their tasks en masse is too great a risk. It therefore seems probable – if only for financial reasons – that these countries will gradually develop more policy programmes in support of carers.

There are currently hints of such developments in all countries: associations of carers (Belgium and the Netherlands), payments to carers, which are however mostly of symbolic amounts (Germany, Belgium, some Departments in France, Luxembourg), easy access to all services for the elderly (Denmark[2]), voluntary "granny-sitting" pools (Germany, Belgium, Netherlands), day centres (all the countries concerned, apart from France where they have practically ceased to exist), temporary residential care (all the countries concerned, but often at the expense of the carer), social holidays organised for elderly dependent persons (France), loans of technical equipment on a free or paying basis (all the countries concerned).[3]

---

1   Today associations of this kind also exist in two other Member States: Belgium and the Netherlands.

2   But, in respect of the Danish concept of caring for dependent people – a State responsibility – no particular attention is paid to carers in the policy programmes.

3   The countries cited in brackets do not constitute an exhaustive list.

It should be remembered that these services and allowances can be very restricted in their scope and distribution within Member States. The most common service of all is concerned with psychological support, listening, advice and information (formal services and self-help groups).

Lastly, as in Great Britain and Ireland, **caring for carers is on the agenda for political discussion,** to differing degrees in all of the northerly countries of the Community.

It would appear that preparatory work for specific programmes is advancing on a practical level in France. The central government, following two reports produced by authoritative political sources[1], is redefining its policy on the elderly, which involves the integration of the third component, caring for carers. There is therefore no longer a policy on the old age which can be summed up, for practical purposes, as a policy of dependence, but instead there is an emerging policy on the elderly and the family.

Caring for carers, either now or in the future, also depends on factors other than community care policies, such as political and ideological ideas, or the economic pressure of the cost of old age on the national budget, for example. It seems that the **absence** or weakness **of pressure groups** constitutes a sort of invitation to laxity among the public authorities and other decision-makers. So long as carers bend silently under the weight of their responsibilities, and bottle up their suffering and anger (with a strong sense of guilt on top of that) their chances of being heard and receiving effective support will remain slim.

Utopia or possible practical advance? According to Alan Walker, improved conditions for community care will undoubtedly be produced in all Member States, but the services will nevertheless remain at a minimal level in most countries. "There is little realistic hope of a

---

1   The National Assembly and the "Commissariat au Plan" [National Planning Commission].

massive (...) growth in home care, for example to harmonise with Danish levels of provision. There is even less chance of voluntary *sponsorship* (...) by national governments, or in the medium term, by the EC Commission. The best that older people (and, one may add, carers) can hope for is that the growing political confidence of older people's organisations in Europe will bear fruit." [Walker, 1991b] If there is a practical advance, this seems to be most noticeable in Britain, relatively negligible in Denmark, and more or less hypothetical - at least in the short if not the medium term - in the other countries of the Community.

When it comes to the recommendations which bring this report to its conclusion, one sees how broad is the field of all that remains to be done, if one wishes to pursue the aim of enabling most care for the dependent elderly to remain in the hands of their families.

A real social policy in favour of carers is a multifaceted and wide-ranging undertaking leading to considerable financial implications for the contributors, public and private, to social programmes.

The *Danish model* teaches us that any social policy for the elderly which claims allegiance to the principle of guaranteeing a decent life for elderly people at home - a principle followed in theory by all Community countries - will inevitably fail to have any impact on the real situation if on the one hand it does not acknowledge the high financial cost which such a choice implies for the nation, and if on the other hand it does not release at the same time the necessary budgets for its application [Pedersen, 1992].

4. Recommendations for a policy in favour of the family carer

Keeping an elderly person at home cannot be done without involving the family and even the neighbours. Neither, however, can it be done without support services. [Neitzert, 1990[

Recommendations are presented, aimed on the one hand to preserve the resource which is provided today by elderly spouses and adult descendants in looking after dependent elderly people at the end of their lives; and on the other hand to argue that socio-political and financial resources should be put in place to provide **effective** and **real** support for those who bear the major burden of care. Although nobody really hopes that they will one day have to bear the burden represented by a dependent parent, the family in all Member States is generally willing and committed to providing care when the need arises. The **challenge is to support this preference and potential through a policy of caring for carers.**

An increase in effective aids for carers would reduce or even eliminate the *"all or nothing"* factor, which is burdensome in itself.

The similarities in the recommendations formulated in the national reports derive logically from similarities in the context of family care, treated at some length in the second part of the present report (attitudes, motivation, burdens, aspirations, needs).

The recommendations are based on the idea that choice must be a basic principle guaranteed to family carers.

All of the recommendations below are not concerned with every country, either because a resource may already exist (for example, the Associations of Carers in the United Kingdom), or because the measure would make no sense (for example, information on assistance for carers where such assistance is non-existent).

The interdependence and interaction between the quality of life of the carer and of the recipient of care mean that a number of the recommendations (deriving from the national reports and repeated here) are not exclusively concerned with carers but have to do with services or supports which are designed in the first place for the elderly person. Directly or indirectly, the existence of these services is also useful to the carer - just as the lack of such services is a disservice to the carer.

Although any improvement in the living conditions of the older elderly has repercussions on the quality of life for their family carers, the recommendations which follow exclude ideas more specifically concerned with the elderly people (for example, gerontological training for professionals), as the present research is expressly **centred on the carer**. The only recommendations mentioned are those directly concerned with maintaining the capacity to care and the quality of life of the carer.

The implementation and financing of these recommendations may be determined, on the one hand, by the laws and systems in force in Members States, while on the other hand they would have to be introduced at several levels: European, national, regional, local. Lastly, certain recommendations are addressed to the public or private decision-makers on social policy, while others are addressed to service-providing associations and organisations or the various voluntary networks, and others again are addressed to the different European institutions, including the Commission. Reference will be made to this factor as far as possible.

I. MEASURES IN FAVOUR OF THE CARER

1. Ensuring that the specific needs and role of the family in caring for the dependent elderly are recognised and made the object of social and political measures which improve the family carer's quality of life on an everyday basis.

Specifically addressed to :
The authorities in charge of social policy for the elderly
The mass media
Carers' associations

2. Establishing social policies for the elderly which include measures for family carers, in order to ensure family-based policies for the elderly.

Practical assistance for family carers should form an integral part of the objectives and responsibilities of services and organisations looking after the elderly.
Small area planning is particularly favourable in this regard, judging from experiments carried out at local level in several Member States.

Specifically addressed to :
The authorities in charge of social policy for the elderly
Carers' associations

3. Promoting, creating or strengthening all forms of respite care.

The more demanding the care situation, as regards stress and time, the more important it is for the carer to be able to get away for an hour, an evening, a day, a weekend, a week, or a month, and it must be possible for him or her to do this in a readily planned way. The carer needs activities and relationships outside the home and outside the care situation, to *recharge the batteries*, to preserve one's own identity as well as one's psychological and physical health, so as to avoid sinking into total immersion in the care situation, and into isolation.

The necessity for such arrangements goes beyond the carer's needs for recuperation, but is also concerned with periods when the recipient of care is incapacitated, through being confined to bed or being hospitalised, for example.

In any case, respite care periods are necessary not only for the carer, but also for the dependent person, who also needs other relationships and the benefits of such relationships have positive effects for the carer too.

There must be no question of creating places where elderly persons are kept in custody and treated like children.

The relief services should be provided at costs which can be met by the financial resources of the people concerned.

There must be specialisation in at least some relief services, for recipients of care affected by mental deterioration.

Remote-control alarm systems, by bringing safety and a sense of security, make it possible to leave the elderly person alone at home.

A number of respite care approaches have worked well in more than one Member State:

[] *"granny-sitting"*
   limited to a few hours;

[] day centres
   providing leisure activities and occupational therapy, health care (nursing and bodily hygiene), movement therapy or exercises, and chiropody, as well as involving the guests in tasks connected with meals: cooking, laying the table, washing up;

[] temporary residential care;

[] holiday stays for dependent people
here again three aspects should be covered: health care, recreation, therapy. For caring spouses, who generally refuse to take separate holidays, the aim is to relieve them of all domestic tasks and care responsibilities, and offer them leisure activities and trips that are not specifically designed for dependent people;

[] temporary "fostering" in a family.
Two kinds may be distinguished:
   . another family member accommodates the elderly relative in;
   . the elderly person is taken to stay (as a paying guest) in the home of a person with whom they have no family links.

Specifically addressed to :
Those who take decisions and provide finance for social policy
Social and health institutions for the elderly
Institutions/centres and people providing holidays for the elderly
Formal networks: associations of carers, voluntary associations, etc.

4. Financial compensation and assistance, direct and indirect, must be ensured, by simplifying the legal arrangements for access to this aid, and the administrative procedures involved.

Such schemes cover a number of aspects:

[] an allowance to recognise the value of work done;

[] financial compensation where occupational activities are reduced or abandoned because of the care situation;

[] financial assistance for temporary housing;

[] coverage of expenses connected with dependence (medical and paramedical costs, including incontinence pads, purchase / rental of minor equipment and technical resources such as wheelchairs, hospital beds, walking frames, etc.).

[] tax allowances for expenses due to the maintenance of the patient in the family, and tax advantages at least for those on low incomes;

Specifically addressed to :
Those who make and take decisions on social policy
Tax legislators

5. Providing sickness and pension coverage for the carer in connection with disability and old age.

All over the Community one finds many cases of poverty caused by the care situation, especially when the carer retires and in old age.

Specifically addressed to :
Social policy decision-makers
Insurance schemes (illness and retirement)

6. Introducing or strengthening the various kinds of housing assistance to carers in order to improve living conditions and care conditions:

[] housing allowance;

[] access to a larger dwelling in cases of co-residence (through the housing allowance);

[] financial assistance for the adaptation of the home to provide increased comfort (hot water, indoor lavatory, central heating, etc.) or to provide increased safety (non-slip flooring, grab bars, etc.).;

Specifically addressed to :
Those who take decisions and provide finance for social policy
Social housing organisations/owners
Public or semi-public organisations for the improvement of housing
conditions

7. **Encouraging and supporting the creation of associations of carers,
both local and national**, particularly modelled on the British
experience (see annex 5). It is of paramount importance that carers
form themselves into **pressure groups**.

Specifically addressed to :
Defence associations / groupings, self-help groups, carers support
groups
Social and political authorities
Professionals in health and social welfare

8. **Introducing a series of specific measures designed for carers
carrying on work activity**, which would give them a real choice about
the various options: remaining in employment, reducing work, stopping
work.

These arrangements should be designed on a similar basis as those which
apply to employees with childcare responsibilities.

-   [] an absolutely necessary condition is access to alternative
    sources of care for the dependent person: to basic assistance,
    nursing care and bodily hygiene care, home help, monitoring,
    access to a day centre.
    For cases of night work or Saturday or Sunday working,
    specific solutions need to be found;

-   [] real transfer of responsibilities during working time - for
    the carer to feel free, he or she must be able to rely
    completely on a person or institution and be summoned only in
    emergencies;

[] establishment of flexible working hours for carers;

[] establishment of paid leave for carers, with coverage of rights to pension and sickness benefits;

[] guaranteed or priority re-employment
given that the end of the situation cannot be planned in advance, this is harder to arrange than maternity leave;

[] accumulation without financial contribution of social insurance rights (illness and old age) on the basis of reduced working time, or in cases where work is given up;

[] options for early retirement
the advantage here seems however to be limited to a few cases (for example at the end of a career or if the caring role is only a minor reason for quitting) on account of the potential negative effects of early retirement (for example, the high financial cost) and because of losing an activity and relationships *outside the care situation* and *outside the home* - in other words, losing a counterweight which balances the care situation.

Specifically addressed to :
Companies
Employees' and employers' unions
Those in charge of legislation in matters of labour law
Insurance schemes (illness and retirement)
Social policy decision-makers

9. Promoting opportunities for para-professional training, counselling and monitoring of carers; helping carers to become aware of their own needs in this area.

Experience of initiatives in Germany, England, Belgium, France, Netherlands, etc. shows that this leads to improvements in the quality of life for carers, and brings them greater satisfaction in the situation and relationship of care.

[] building up practical knowledge and skills,
for daily procedures (how to lift the person from their bed,
from a sitting position, or somebody who has fallen on the
floor; how to give a bath or shower; how to change the sheets
while the person is in bed). More professionalism makes the
tasks easier, provides a sense of security, and improves the
quality of care.
Such teaching could be provided by the professionals in the
field, by hospitals while the recipient of care is an in-
patient, and by organisations such as the Red Cross;

[] monitoring the successive phases in the care situation
each stage of development has its own specific features, not
only in cases of dementia; the carer must not be stranded in
crisis situations requiring decisions, new arrangements, new
psychological approaches.
The *post-care* phase needs preparation and monitoring, whether
the situation has come to an end because the elderly person
has died, or because they have gone into a residential
institution.
The carer also needs to learn to see a possible admission to
residential care in terms **other than the usual negative image
of residential institutions, and other than as a cause of
guilty feelings.**

[] emotional/psychological support
the unsatisfied needs to talk, to express one's rage and
suffering, to weep, to be listened to and heard without value-
judgements, are of enormous importance.
Carers also have to learn how to **establish and negotiate their
own limitations,** to keep their distance, to **preserve
themselves;** many simply need to learn how to laugh again; they
need to learn not to get stressed pointlessly, and to avoid
getting into *bad habits* which are difficult to undo; they need
to learn how to communicate with the recipient of care about
the difficulties of the care situation.

Specifically addressed to :
Community care services/associations
Hospitals, day centres/clinics
Organisations such as the Red Cross
Associations of carers, associations of families, etc.; local carers'
networks; associations / services for the elderly
Those who take decisions and provide finance for social policy

10. Promoting information for carers. Information must cover, in
particular, the social services both formal and informal, the
neighbourhood networks, associations, and support groups; the aids and
financial benefits; it must cover the rights of carers; it must cover
the illness from which the older person is suffering, and how this may
change over time.
This type of information is generally too fragmented.

Many ways of providing information, have been tried out in different
Member States, for example:

[] the print media, production of catalogues of rights and aids,
production of guides for carers;

[] television programmes (on the lines followed by the British
television);

[] other mass media;

[] telephone services providing advice, information and more
active counselling and listening (these may be manned by
volunteers);

[] local advice centres providing both local information and
personal advice;

[] general medical practitioners and geriatricians (at their
surgeries, in hospitals, at home) - doctors themselves must
become more aware and active around the problems of carers and
possible solutions;

[] contact services for carers; district information contact points.

Specifically addressed to :
The medical profession
Mass media
Associations of carers, associations such as the Alzheimer's Association or the Parkinson's Association, support groups, etc.
Insurance schemes
Social services of local authorities

11. Encouraging the development of support groups, which have the reputation almost of a panacea in gerontological circles, because their results are generally so positive, especially when there is some professional backup. Experience in different Member States tends to prove that psychological support, when interspersed with information, is more acceptable to participants than psychological sessions on their own; it should be specified that these groups do not carry out psychotherapy.

Specifically addressed to :
Associations of carers, contact services for carers; associations / social services for the elderly
The medical and paramedical professions
Mass media
Insurance schemes (especially for illness)
Those who take decisions and provide finance for social policy

12. Including instruction on the specific problems of carers within professional training for all those involved, including doctors.

The carer needs to be more fully understood by the professionals and their support structures, and should thereby receive more effective support. Professionals also require skills to train family carers.

Specifically addressed to :

Those responsible for the initial training and the in-service training (specialist and advanced courses) for professionals concerned with the elderly.

13. Facilitating access to technical support and equipment support.

[]   rental of paramedical equipment and machinery
      hospital bed, wheelchair or walking-frame for example, where
      the high purchase price may exceed the means of the family, or
      the family may hesitate in spending the money for fear that it
      would only be used for a short time.
      This equipment must be in perfect working order.

[]   telephone (at a reduced tariff) in the carer's home and, if
      the carer is not residing with the recipient of care, in that
      person's home also;

[]   tele-alarm system
      what is proposed here is on the one hand a remote-controlled
      system, with the elderly person wearing an alarm button, and
      on the other hand a system utilising neighbourhood
      networks.[1]

      This audio coverage of the home also has a reassuring function
      both for the elderly person and for the carer, who can leave
      the home without worrying. The system should provide night-
      time monitoring if there is not a situation of co-residence.

Specifically addressed to :
Rental organisations/services
Insurance schemes (illness)
Community care services/associations
Those who take decisions and provide finance for social policy

---

1   When the switchboard receives a call, it dispatches a member of the voluntary network according to the needs of the caller, and only sends specialist personnel when it is really necessary.

14. Developing policies and practices in favour of carers belonging to ethnic minorities would be necessary wherever an area has a certain number of immigrants who have held on to the traditions or religious practices of their country of origin.

Specifically addressed to :
Those who take decisions and provide finance for social policy
Immigrants associations
Community care services/associations

15. Eliminating, as far as possible, violence. The veil of discretion which covers the question of violence between the carer and the recipient of care (as well as between the carer and other family members) means that the real situation with regard to this topic is poorly understood and hushed up.

Specifically addressed to :
Those who take decisions and provide finance for social policy
Mass media
Carers associations; family associations
The medical and paramedical professions
Support groups
Community care services/associations

16. Promoting and ensuring the development of social research about family carers so as to make good the obvious gaps in all European Community countries in our knowledge of the socio-demographic and socio-cultural characteristics of carers, the actual work which they do and their needs.

These gaps undermine the reliability of any precise evaluation of the impact of existing aid programmes, the needs for assistance, and by implication any forecasting of the costs and expenses which may be expected.

One of the subjects which should be covered by research is the reasons for *non-participation by males,* which is very widespread among descendants.

Specifically addressed to :
Those who take decisions and provide finance for social policy
Social-gerontologic research institutes and those who provide finance for such research

II. MEASURES IN FAVOUR OF THE ELDERLY PERSON AND THE CARER

17. **Creating, extending and/or restructuring home services;** in addition to running them flexibly and seven days a week, this has to do with **practical assistance,** particularly of a domestic kind, and **home nursing,** including personal hygiene. The number of hours and the number of interventions must be decided on the basis of the actual needs, which are variable, of the elderly person and of the carer.

These services must not be reserved for the older elderly living on their own: carers must have access to them when they are co-resident with the person being cared for; older people living alone must have access to them even if they are being cared for by their family.

Specifically addressed to :
Those who take decisions and provide finance for social policy

18. **Systematically reinforcing co-operation between the different people supporting the dependent person, including the principal carer,** around the patients needs and based on those needs; this co-ordination should *go without saying* because of the complementary nature of the supports. It is a matter of negotiating clearly *who* does *what,* taking account of each person's possibilities and the development in needs brought about by any change in the situation on the part of the patient or the carer. The dependent older person must be a participant both in

negotiating who does what and in co-ordination, so as to maintain the maximum level of autonomy.

Such co-operation - or other forms of assistance made to measure - would lead to co-ordination between different services and reduce the division between social and health concerns.

Specifically addressed to :
Those who take decisions and provide finance for social policy
Those in charge of community care services
All those actively involved

19. Developing innovative institutional accommodation for elderly people affected by psychological deterioration

An example here are the small units which exist in France, taking in about a dozen patients and integrating active family help in daily living.

This mode of accommodation lies at the margins of caring for carers, because this method of looking after patients can mean the end of a care situation. Nevertheless, its urgency derives from the particularly onerous problems of this type of care.

Specifically addressed to :
Those who take decisions and provide finance for social policy
Carers' associations
Property investors, public and private, specialising in providing collective housing for elderly people

20. Paying attention to changes and encouraging those changes which are working towards a greater interpenetration between sectors of activity: the public sector, the private sector, the family, voluntary organisations / networks (tendencies towards a *welfare mix*).

Specifically addressed to :
Those who take decisions on social policy

III.   MEASURES IN FAVOUR OF THE CARER, FOR THE SPECIFIC ATTENTION OF EUROPEAN BODIES, PARTICULARLY THE EUROPEAN COMMISSION

It is noted that several international organisations, such as the Council of Europe and the International Labour Office, have made explicit reference to the needs of carers of older people, specifically in relation to issues of social protection and employment. It is recognised that the Commission of the European Communities must respect the subsidiarity principle and therefore undertake only those tasks which can, by reason of the scale or effects of the proposed action, be achieved more effectively at Community level. Nevertheless, the Member States of the Community face common challenges associated with ageing of the population and the needs for care of the dependent elderly. These challenges to provision of care are likely to strengthen in the context of the changing role of women in the labour market; migration, including that of older people, between Member States; financial pressures on the formal welfare service; and the expectations of care services held by the next generation of older people and their families. In considering what can usefully be achieved at European level, it will be important to assess the potential of legislative or regulatory approaches through EC competencies in relation, for example, to the equal treatment of men and women; but there are also important opportunities to employ diverse instruments to stimulate research, training, public information, policy development, and education. European bodies may contribute to improving quality of life for older people and their carers through :

21. Preparing and securing official recognition for a Carers' Charter, like those developed already in Ireland and the Netherlands. Such a Charter, perhaps in the form of a Recommendation from the Council of EC Ministers, would emphasise the rights and needs of carers and would define objectives to be achieved, acknowledging though that different countries will adopt approaches consistent with their own systems and cultures.

22. Preparing and financing specific action and assistance programmes for carers which would contribute to the transfer of knowledge and innovation. A network of pilot or demonstration projects could be established, using the EC's poverty programmes as a model. This would underline the importance of European support for the development and evaluation of innovatory action at local level; such projects could, for example look at strengthening the contribution to caring made through neighbourhood organisations, community groups and other local networks.

23. Encouraging the creation of a European network of national carers' organisations which would facilitate learning and advocacy. In most countries these associations are as yet under discussion or in the process of being established. These groups need support to meet, to develop their organisation and to communicate with non-governmental organisations representing congruent interests at international level. Insofar as such associations would find it useful to establish a European union, they could contribute to debate in various EC forums (and have a role in monitoring the success of these recommendations).

24. Proclaiming a Carers' Day in 1994 within the context of the Year of the Family (United Nations), as an important element in improving recognition of family carers and the contribution they make, both socially and economically. This Carers' Day could build upon the experience and networks established for events during the European Year of Older People and Solidarity between the Generations.

25. Publicising the responsibilities, activities and burdens assumed by the family for dependent older relatives as a means of increasing awareness of the role of the family in care. This important task will be done most effectively with the support of non-governmental and local organisations, but a document from the Commission, such as a Communication, would trigger reflection and political discussion among key interest groups such as the social partners, service providers and other organisations at local, national and European levels.

26. Stimulating and supporting Member States to develop policies and actions for carers and for elderly people, on the basis of experience in other countries. This involves a structure and medium for the exchange of experiences, and the fostering of action networks. Such networks must include public, private and voluntary organisations with experience in the development and delivery of services to carers.

27. Encouraging the development of training programmes and opportunities for voluntary and professional workers, who can and do provide support to family carers. There is an urgent need to increase awareness and skills of those who help, and may train, carers. Considering the scale of the problem and the unmet need for trained workers, it may be possible to identify resources in the Social Fund or in other parts of the Structural Funds, intended to enhance the social dimension of the internal market.

28. Promoting systematic research on the situation of family carers and measures to improve this, as a basis for informed debate and appropriate planning. In some Member States the lack of basic information about family care must be addressed, while in general there is a lack of information on the effects of existing initiatives and policies on the quality of life of family carers. There is a need for information on the costs and effectiveness of public policies for care of older people, but also on the economic value of care by families, and the economic costs to those families. Current EC research programmes, such as those on technology, should consider applications to support carers as well as older people.

29. Ensuring that the needs and interests of family carers of older people are taken into account in the development of EC programmes and actions. This may be especially important for initiatives to stimulate employment and training, not only because of the need for skilled, paid home care workers, but also because many family carers were, are, or want to be in paid employment - with implications therefore for social security protection, public and company policies to combine employment and caring, and training or re-training initiatives. The monitoring and promotion of carers' interests thus engages the social partners and a wide spectrum of non-governmental organisations, as well as the institutions of the European Community.

A final word ...

In the countries of the Community, with some rare exceptions, there is an imbalance, as surprising as it is unacceptable, between, on the one hand, the fact that the family is the leading *world institution* for looking after dependent people at home, and on the other hand the very limited degree of attention and consideration given to the family by the public and, even more seriously, by those people who take decisions on social policy and social action.

This family production cannot be replaced by formal services provided by paid professionals: in the current state of social legislation, of the financial resources for social expenditure, or indeed the design of national budgets, no Member State is remotely able or willing to substitute for family care. Notwithstanding this, one cannot rule out the possibility that the family's commitment for this task might diminish; if there were a major quantitative reduction in this resource – a social **risk** being run by European societies which could, in the years to come, be transformed into a social **reality** – who would replace the family carer?

It is unlikely that this family production of care will remain at the very high level of today **if the carers do not receive the assistance and support which they urgently need**, or if they fail to obtain the recognition and respect which a society calling itself a Welfare State owes to them.

Laxity by governments in dealing with this topic, and failure to introduce social policies for carers, constitute a very high-risk policy for tomorrow's community, because we are today, and we will be tomorrow, demographically very old societies. The *grey* society of the twenty-first century is now being constructed. Current policies are staking out the form of that society in an irrevocable fashion.

ANNEXES

References [1]

AUDIRAC Pierre-Alain, 1985 : *Les personnes âgées, de la vie de famille à l'isolement.* in Economie et Statistiques, n° 175, mars 85, INSEE, Paris, pp. 39-54.

BALDOCK John, EVERS Adalbert, 1991 : Innovations and Care of the Elderly : *The Front Line of Change for Social Welfare Services,* in Aging International, Vol. XVIII, N° 1, June, 1991, Washington, pp. 3-21.

BAUER-SÖLLNER B., 1991 : *Institutionen der offenen Altenhilfe - aktueller Stand und Entwicklungstendenzen,* in Expertisen zum ersten Teilbericht der Sachverständigenkommission zur Erstellung des ersten Altenberichts der Bundesregierung. DZA, Berlin, pp. 57-234.

BETTELHEIM Bruno, 1970 : *L'Amour ne suffit pas. Le traitement des troubles affectifs chez l'enfant.* Editions Fleurus, collection Pédagogie psychosociale, Paris.

BRAUN Hans, 1991 : *Critical events in informal care : a process-related approach,* paper presented at the European Conference on Informal Care, University of York, 23-25 September 1991. Proceedings, to be published.

BRISEPIERRE Christine, 1987 : *Une approche des solidarités familiales : La cohabitation enfants-parents âgés.* Mémoire, I.F.P.T.S., Dijon.

BRODY Elaine, 1985 : *Parent care as a normative family stress,* in The Gerontologist, 25/1.

BRUCKLER-DAMJANOVIC G., 1991 : *Premier bilan socio-démographique sur la situation des personnes âgées au Grand-Duché de Luxembourg,* in Revue d'Action Sociale, n° 4, juillet-août 91, Liège, pp. 72-81.

CHRISTINE Marc, SAMY Christian, 1988 : *L'équipement des ménages en biens durables : évolutions et situation à la mi-86.* Collections de l'INSEE, Série M no. 135, nov. 88. INSEE, Paris.

COX Carole, 1991 : *Community Care : Expanding the Griffiths Report,* in Aging International, Vol. XVIII, N° 1, June 91, Washington, p. 12.

DELL'ORTO Frederica, TACCANI Patricia : *Family caregiver and dependent elderly in Italy : a first analysis,* paper prepared for the European Conference on Informal Care, University of York, 23-25 September 1991. Proceedings, to be published.

DIECK Margret, 1991 : *Die Vernachlässigung der ambulanten und häuslichen Versorgung alter Menschen in der Bundesrepublik Deutschland hat System und ist systembedingt,* in Die soziale Arbeit in den 90ger Jahren. Neue Herausforderungen bei offenen Grenzen in Europa. Schriften des Deutschen Vereins für öffentliche und private Fürsorge, Frankfurt am Main, pp. 432-451.

EBERHARD Serge, HARDT Ilse, THYES Jules, THOMA Franz, WISELER Claude (1992) : *Programme National pour Personnes Agées, Ministère de la famille et de la solidarité,* Luxembourg, 1992.

ESPACE SOCIAL EUROPEEN (anonymous), 1991 : *Aperçu de la protection médico-sociale des personnes âgées en Europe.* Dossier spécial. N° 1, jnv. 91, O.E.P.S. Editeur, Paris.

---

[1] Please note that this list — with some exceptions — contains only works which are not included in the references in the national reports.

Annex 1

European Foundation for the Improvement of Living and Working Conditions (anonymous), 1989 : *Four Rolling Programme 1989-1992. 1992 and beyong : New opportunities for action to improve living and working conditions in Europe.* Office for Official Publications of the European Communities, Luxemburg.

EUROSTAT (anonymous), 1988 : *Censuses of Population in the Community countries 1981-1982.* Statistical Office of the European Communities, Luxemburg.

EUROSTAT (anonymous), 1990 : *Demographic Statistics.* Statistical Office of the European Communities, Luxemburg.

EUROSTAT (anonymous), 1991 : *Demographic Statistics.* Statistical Office of the European Communities, Luxemburg.

EVANDROU Maria, 1990 : *Care for the Elderly in Britain*, paper presented at the Scientific Colloquium, 24 March 1990 in Brussels.

EVERS Adalbert, 1991 : *Diversity and Transition — The Interactions of professional and informal Helpers in home-based Care Services for the Elderly,* paper presented at the European Conference on Informal Care, University of York, 23-25 September 1991. Proceedings, to be published.

EVERS Adalbert, 1992 : *Megatrends im Wohlfahrtsmix. Soziale Dienstleistungen zwischen Deregulierung und Neugestaltung,* in Blätter der Wohlfahrtspflege — Deutsche Zeitschrift für Sozialarbeit, Jan. 92, pp. 3-7.

FACCHINI Carla, 1991 : *Risk and achievements in strengthening home-care for elderly people : the Italian situation*, paper presented at the International Conference : Better care for dependent people living at home : Meeting the new agenda in services for the elderly, Noordwijkerhout, Netherlands, November 28-30, 1991. Proceedings, to be published.

FINCH Janet, 1991 : *The concept of caring : Femnist and other perspectives*, paper for the European Conference on Informal Care, University of York, 23-25 September 1991. Proceedings, to be published

Fondation de France Edt. 1988 : *Les Cantou en question. Des petites unités de vie communautaire pour les personnes âgées dépendantes.* Actes de la journée de réflexion du 28 avril 1988, Paris.

FRIIS H., 1991 : *New Directions in Policies for the Elderly in Europe*, in European Journal of Gerontology, Vol. 1, N° 2, Nov. 91, pp. 42-49.

GUILLEMARD Anne-Marie, PITAUD Philippe, 1991 : *Les politiques sociales et économiques de gestion du vieillissement en France.* Rapport national pour la CE D.G. V, Paris.

HOLSTEIN Bjørn E., 1991 : *Formal and informal care for the Elderly : Lessons from Denmark,* paper presented at the International Conference : Better care for dependent people living at home : Meeting the new agenda in services for the elderly, Noordwijkerhout, Netherlands, November 28-30, 1991. Proceedings, to be published.

INFRATEST (anonymous), 1991a : *Hilfebedarf und Behinderungen bei Alltagsaktivitäten in ausgewählten Bevölkerungsgruppen. Sekundäranalysen über Möglichkeiten und Grenzen selbständiger Lebensführung.* Berichtsband. Infratest Sozialforschung, Infratest Gesundheitsforschung, München.

INFRATEST (anonymous), 1991b : *Möglichkeiten und Grenzen selbständiger Lebensführung. Ergebnisse der Testerhebungen* (2. Zwischenbericht). Infratest Sozialforschung, Infratest Gesundheitsforschung, München.

JAMIESON Anne, 1991 : *Care for people living at home : A European Perspective*, draft paper for the International Conference : Better care for dependent people living at home : Meeting the new agenda in services for the elderly, Noordwijkerhout, Netherlands, November 28-30, 1991. Proceedings, to be published.

Annex 1

JANI-LE BRIS Hannelore, 1990a : *Définir une résidence "idéale" pour retraités. I. Rapport de synthèse, II. volume de tableaux*, Enquête Cleirppa, unpublished, Paris.

JANI-LE BRIS Hannelore, 1990b: *Les bénéficiaires ruraux d'une aide ménagère ADMR : I. Rapport national, II. Volume de tableaux*, Enquête Cleirppa, unpublished, Paris.

JANI-LE BRIS Hannelore, 1991 : *La personne âgée dans son quartier*. Enquête Cleirppa, unpublished, Paris.

JANI-LE BRIS Hannelore, LUQUET Valérie, 1992 : *Grand âge et perte d'autonomie. I. Rapport de synthèse, II. Volume de tableaux*. Etude Cleirppa, unpublished, Paris.

KASTELEIN Maarten, DIJKSTRA A., SCHOUTEN C.C., 1989 : *Care of the elderly in the Netherlands: a review of policies and services 1950-1990*. Institut of Preventive Health Care, Leiden.

KRAAN Robbert J., BALDOCK John, DAVIES Bleddyn, EVERS Adalbert, JOHANSSON Lennarth, KNAPEN Martin, THORSLUND Mats, TUNISSEN Catherine, 1991 : *Care for the Elderly. Significant Innovations in three European Countries*. European Centre for Social Welfare Policy and Research, Vol. 6, Campus/Westview, Frankfurt/Main and Boulder, Colorado.

KDA (anonymous), 1991 : *Wie viele Menschen leben im Heim ?* in KDA Presse- und Informationsdienst, Folge 5/1991, Köln, p. 4.

KDA (anonymous), 1992 : *Pflegende Angehörige zwischen Pflege und Beruf - Wie Unternehmen helfen könnem*, in KDA Presse- und Informationsdienst, Folge 1/1992, Köln, pp. 5-6.

KINSELLA Kevin, 1990 : *Suicide at Older Ages : An International Enigma*, in Aging International, vol. XVII, n° 2, Winter 1990, Washington, pp. 36-38.

LEPINE Nicole, NOBECOURT Marie-Pascale, 1991 : *Lexique à l'usage des néophytes*, in Etre vieux. De la négation à l'échange, Ed. Autrement, série Mutations, n° 124, oct. 91, Paris, pp. 76-83.

LORIAUX Michel, 1989 : *Les populations européennes face à la révolution grise : Dimensions démographiques et sociales d'une mutation de société*, in Les Apports des Personnes âgées à la Société européenne, I.E.I.A.S., Marcinelle (Belgium).

METZ Ursula, DIERL Reinhard, 1984 : *Wohngemeinschaften älterer Menschen*. KDA, Köln.

NIJKAMP Peter, PACOLET Jozef, SPINNEWYN Hilde, VOLLERING Ans, WILDEROM Celeste, WINTERS Sien, 1991 : *Les services d'aides aux personnes âgées en Europe. Une étude comparative entre les différents pays de la CEE*. HIVA, Louvain.

O'CONNOR Joyce, RUDDLE Helen, 1988 : *Caring for the elderly, part II. The caring process : a study of carers in the home*. National Council for the Aged, report no. 19, Dublin.

OTTO Ulrich, 1992 : *Über Arbeitsplatz und Ehrenamt hinaus. Sozialpolitische Herausforderungen der Erwerbsgesellschaft*, in Blätter der Wohlfahrtspflege — Deutsche Zeitschrift für Sozialarbeit, Jan. 92, pp. 7-11.

O'SHEA Eamon, 1991 : *The Impact of Social and Economic Policies on Older People in Ireland*. National report for the EC D.G. V, Galway.

PARANT Alain, 1990 : *Le vieillissement en Europe*, in Les Actes des Rencontres départementales de Gérontologie sociale, Marseille, 19 et 20 octobre 1989, Conseil Général des Bouches-du-Rhône, Marseille.

PARKER Gillian, 1985 : *With due care and attention. A review of research on informal care*. Family Policy Studies Centre, London.

Annex 1

PEDERSEN Ole Ryan, 1993 : *Altenpflege in Dänemark — ein Modell für Europa auch für den ländlichen Raum ?* in HOWE Jürgen (Hrsg.) : *Alternpflege auf dem Lande. Perspektiven und Entwicklungen in Westeuropa*, Asanger, Heidelberg, pp. 14-24.

PEREZ ORTIZ Lourdes, 1991 (année présumée) : *La situation des personnes âgées en Espagne et les politiques de vieillesse en Espagne.* Rapport national pour la CE D.G. V.

PLOVSING Jan, 1991 : *Zehn Jahre Erfahrungen in der Hausbetreuung der Aelteren in Dänemark.* IVSS, ISSA , AISS, Paris.

ROSENMAYR Leopold, 1988 : *Die Gefahren des Beherrschens in der Pflege oder die Freuden der «sehenden» Hilfe*, in Mitteilungen zur Altenhilfe, 25 Jahrgang, 4. Vierteljahr 88, Frankfurt/Main, pp. 3-12.

ROSENMAYR Leopold, 1990 : *Die Kräfte des Alters*, Edition Atelier, Wien.

SCHMIDT-NIELSEN Bjarne, 1991 : *Was sind die wichtigsten Zunkunftsfragen der Alterspolitik und in welchem Zeithorizont müßten sie entschieden werden ?* Podiumsdiskussion Runde III im Freudenstädter Forum am 4. und 5. Oktober 1991 : Solidarität der Generationen : Perspectiven des Alterwerdens der Gesellschaft in Deutschland and Europa. FEA-Manuskripte, Fritz Erler Akademie Freudenstadt.

STEINER-HUMMEL Irene, 1988 : *Angehörigenarbeit in Einrichtungen der Altenhilfe*, in Archiv für Wissenschaft und Praxis der sozialen Arbeit, Nr. 3/88, Frankfurt, pp. 198-211.

THIEDE Reinhard, 1986 : *Die Situation von Privathaushalten mit pflegebedürftigen Haushaltsmitgliedern. Ansätze einer empirischen Analyse für die Bundesrepublik Deutschland.* Based upon *Pflegende Angehörige zwischen Pflege und Beruf — Wie Unternehmen helfen können* (anonymous), in KDA Presse- und Informationsdienst, Folge 1/92, Köln, pp. 5 et 6.

THIEDE Reinhard, 1988 : *Die besondere Lage der älteren Pflegebedürftigen. Empirische Analysen und sozialpolitische Überlegungen auf der Basis aktuellen Datenmaterials*, in Sozialer Fortschritt, Nr 37, Nov. 88, pp. 250-255.

TUNISSEN Catherine, KNAPEN Mat, 1991 : *The National Context of Social Innovation — The Netherlands*, in [KRAAN et al., 1991 : 20-27].

URLAUB Karl-Heinz (Hrsg.), 1991 : *Hilfen für pflegende Angehörige. Erfahrungen in der Beratung und in der therapeutischen Gruppenarbeit.* Der Paritätische Wohlfahrtsverband, Wuppertal.

WALKER Alan, 1991a : *The Relationship between the Family and the State in the Care of Older People*, in Canadian Journal on Aging, vol. 10, n° 2, pp. 94-112.

WALKER Alan, 1991b : *Towards a European Agenda in Home Care for Older People : Convergencies and Controversies*, paper presented at the International Conference : Better care for dependent people living at home : Meeting the new agenda in services for the elderly, Noordwijkerhout, Netherlands, November 28-30, 1991. Proceedings, to be published.

WALKER Alan, undated : *Home care in Europe : Current trends and future prospects.* European Association of Organizations for Home Care and help at home, Brussels.

WALKER Alan, GUILLEMARD Anne-Marie, ALBER Jens, 1991 : *Les Politiques sociales et économiques et les Personnes âgées. Premier Rapport Annuel de l'Observatoire de la Communauté Européenne.* Commission des Communautés Européennes, D.G.V, Bruxelles.

ZIOMAS Dimitris, 1991 : *The elderly in Greece : a review of their current situation with reference to social and economic policies.* National report for the EC, Athens.

155

National Reports

B   George **Hedebouw**
HIVA — Hoger Instituut voor de Arbeid. Katholieke Universiteit
E. Van Evenstraat 2E - B-3000 Leuven

D   Hanneli **Döhner**, Herbert **Rüb**, Birgit **Schick**
Universität Hamburg - Institut für Medizin-Soziologie - Schwerpunkt Sozialgerontologie
Martinistraβe 52 - D-2000 Hamburg 20

DK   Poul **Scou**, Eva **Tufte**, George W **Leeson**
EGV - Aeldre Fonden
Vesterbrogade 97 - DK-1620 København V

E   Josep A **Rodriguez-Diaz**
Universidad de Barcelona - Facultad de Econòmicas
Avda. Diagonal 690 - E-08034 Barcelona

F   Hannelore **Jani-Le Bris**
CLEIRPPA - Centre de Liaison, d'Etude, d'Information et de Recherche sur les Problèmes des Personnes Agées
15 Rue Chateaubriand - F-75008 Paris

GR   Judith **Triantafillou**, Elizabeth **Mestheneos**
SEXTANT
Aktaioy 9A - GR-118 51 Athens

IRL   Joyce **O'Connor**
National College of Industrial Relations
Sandford Road - Ranelagh - Dublin 6

I   Massimo **Mengani**, Cristina **Gagliardi**
INRCA - Centro Studi Economico-Sociali
Scalone S. Francesco n° 3 - I-60121 Ancona

NL   Mariëtte **Steenvoorden**
NIZW Nederlands Instituut voor Zorg en Welzijn
Catharijnesingel 47 - NL-3501 DD Utrecht

P   Maria de Lourdes Baptista **Quaresma**
Direçao Municipal de Habitaçao Social
R. Castilho 213 - P-1000 Lisboa

UK   Janet **Finch**, Richard **Hugman**
University of Lancaster - Applied Social Sience
Lancaster LA1 4YW

Research Manager : Robert **Anderson**
European Foundation for the Improvement of Living and Working Conditions

T 1 **Total population and older population of Member States, at 1 January 1989 :**
number (000s) and proportion

	total population N = 100 %	≥ 65 years N	%	≥ 75 years N	%
B	9 927.6	1 450.5	14.6	653.4	6.6
DK	5 129.8	795.8	15.5	350.7	6.8
D [1]	61 715.1	9 515.0	15.4	4 561.9	**7.4**
E	38 851.9	5 036.0	13.0	2 078.6	5.4
F	56 017.0	7 727.9	13.8	3 770.9	6.7
GR	10 019.0	1 373.5	13.7	609.5	6.1
IRL	3 521.8	394.4	**11.1**	154.4	**4.4**
I	57 504.7	8 113.1	14.1	3 516.2	6.1
LUX	374.9	50.1	13.4	22.3	5.9
NL	14 805.2	1 877.0	12.7	793.7	5.4
P [2]	10 304.8	1 325.4	12.9	531.7	5.2
UK	57 150.5	8 918.4	**15.6**	3 892.2	6.8
EUR 12	325 323.3	46 577.5	14.3	20 935.9	6.4

Source : EUROSTAT, 1991 ; based upon table B-4.

[1] before reunification.
[2] provisional data.

Annex 3
Expectation of life
at certain ages (years)

T 2

Espérance de vie
à certains âges (années)

Sex / Sexe	Year / Année	Age / Âge										
		0	1	10	20	30	40	50	60	65	70	75
						EUR 12[*]						
Males	1950	..	..	..	..	..	..	..	..	..	..	..
Hommes	1960	67.3	..	..	..	..	..	..	..	..	..	..
	1970	68.5	..	..	..	..	..	..	..	..	..	..
	1980	70.7	..	..	..	..	..	..	..	..	..	..
	1989	72.8										
Females	1950	..	..	.:	..	..	..	..	..	..	..	..
Femmes	1960	72.7	..	..	..	..	..	..	..	..	..	..
	1970	74.8	..	..	..	..	..	..	..	..	..	..
	1980	77.4	..	..	..	..	..	..	..	..	..	..
	1989	79.2										
						B						
Males	1950	62.0	65.3	57.4	48.0	39.3	30.6	22.5	15.5	12.3	9.5	7.1
Hommes	1960	67.7	68.4	59.9	50.3	40.9	31.7	22.9	15.5	12.4	9.7	7.3
	1970	67.8	68.4	59.9	50.3	40.9	31.6	22.8	15.2	12.1	9.5	7.3
	1980	70.0	70.0	61.2	51.6	42.3	33.0	24.1	16.3	13.0	10.0	7.6
	1989[*]	72.4	72.0	63.2	53.5	44.1	34.7	25.7	17.5	14.0	10.8	8.2
Females	1950	67.3	69.7	61.7	52.3	43.2	34.2	25.5	17.5	13.9	10.7	8.0
Femmes	1960	73.5	73.9	65.3	55.5	45.9	36.3	27.2	18.7	14.8	11.4	8.4
	1970	74.2	74.5	65.9	56.1	46.4	36.9	27.3	19.2	15.3	11.8	8.8
	1980	76.8	76.6	67.9	58.1	48.4	38.8	29.6	20.9	16.9	13.2	9.8
	1989[*]	79.0	78.5	69.7	59.8	50.1	40.5	31.2	22.4	18.2	14.3	10.8
						DK						
Males	1951-55	69.8	71.1	62.7	53.0	43.7	34.3	25.4	17.4	13.9	10.7	8.0
Hommes	1961-62	70.4	71.1	62.6	52.9	43.4	34.0	25.0	17.1	13.7	10.6	7.9
	1970-71	70.1	71.0	62.4	52.8	43.3	33.8	25.0	17.1	13.7	10.8	8.3
	1980	71.4	71.0	62.3	52.6	43.2	33.8	24.9	17.0	13.6	10.7	8.2
	1989[*]	72.0	71.7	62.9	53.1	43.6	34.3	25.4	17.6	14.2	11.2	8.6
Females	1951-55	72.6	73.4	64.8	55.0	45.3	35.9	26.9	18.4	14.6	11.2	8.3
Femmes	1961-62	74.4	74.8	66.1	56.3	46.5	37.0	27.9	19.3	15.3	11.8	8.7
	1970-71	75.9	75.9	67.2	57.4	47.7	38.1	29.1	20.6	16.7	13.1	9.9
	1980	77.2	76.8	68.0	58.2	48.4	38.9	29.8	21.5	17.6	13.9	10.6
	1989[*]	77.7	77.3	68.5	58.6	48.8	39.2	30.1	21.8	17.9	14.4	11.1
						D						
Males	1949-51	64.6	67.8	59.8	50.3	41.3	32.3	23.8	16.2	12.8	9.8	7.3
Hommes	1960-62	66.9	68.3	59.9	50.3	41.1	31.9	23.1	15.5	12.4	9.6	7.2
	1970-72	67.4	68.2	59.7	50.2	41.0	31.8	23.1	15.3	12.1	9.4	7.2
	1980-82	70.2	70.1	61.4	51.8	42.4	33.1	24.3	16.5	13.1	10.1	7.6
	1989[*]	72.6	72.2	63.4	53.7	44.2	34.7	25.8	17.8	14.2	11.1	8.4
Females	1949-51	68.5	71.0	62.8	53.2	43.9	34.7	25.8	17.5	13.7	10.4	7.7
Femmes	1960-62	72.4	73.5	64.9	55.2	45.5	36.1	27.0	18.5	14.6	11.1	8.2
	1970-72	73.8	74.3	65.7	56.0	46.3	36.8	27.7	19.1	15.2	11.6	8.6
	1980-82	76.9	76.7	67.9	58.1	48.4	38.8	29.5	20.8	16.8	13.0	9.7
	1989[*]	79.0	78.5	69.7	59.8	50.1	40.4	31.1	22.2	18.0	14.2	10.7

Expectation of life
at certain ages (years)

Espérance de vie
à certains âges (années)

Sex Sexe	Year Année	Age Âge										
		0	1	10	20	30	40	50	60	65	70	75
							GR					
Males	1950	63.4	66.8	59.6	50.2	41.2	32.3	23.7	16.2	13.0	10.2	7.8
Hommes	1960	67.3	70.3	62.4	52.8	43.4	34.1	25.0	16.9	13.4	10.3	7.7
	1970	70.1	72.2	63.8	54.1	44.6	35.1	25.9	17.5	13.9	10.6	7.9
	1980	72.2	72.8	64.1	54.5	45.0	35.6	26.4	18.2	14.6	11.5	8.8
	1985	72.6	72.9	64.2	54.5	45.1	35.6	22.2	18.2	14.5	11.3	8.4
Females	1950	66.7	69.8	62.4	53.0	43.9	34.8	26.1	18.0	14.4	11.1	8.3
Femmes	1960	70.4	73.2	65.2	55.5	45.9	36.4	27.1	18.6	14.8	11.4	8.5
	1970	73.6	75.3	66.9	57.1	47.4	37.8	28.3	19.3	15.3	11.7	8.4
	1980	76.6	77.0	68.2	58.4	48.7	39.0	29.5	20.6	16.7	13.2	10.3
	1985	77.6	77.8	69.0	59.1	49.4	39.6	30.2	21.1	16.9	12.9	9.4
							E					
Males	1950	59.8	63.2	56.6	47.4	39.0	30.4	22.2	14.9	11.8	9.2	6.8
Hommes	1960	67.4	69.4	61.3	51.7	42.3	33.1	25.2	16.5	13.1	10.2	7.6
	1970	69.2	70.4	61.8	52.2	42.8	33.5	24.7	16.8	13.3	10.3	7.9
	1980	72.5	72.5	63.9	54.2	44.8	35.4	26.4	18.4	14.8	11.5	8.8
	1987*	73.2	73.2	64.4	54.8	45.4	36.0	27.1	18.9	15.4	12.0	9.2
Females	1950	64.3	67.3	60.7	51.6	42.8	33.9	25.3	17.1	13.5	10.3	7.6
Femmes	1960	72.2	73.7	65.5	55.8	46.2	36.8	27.7	19.2	15.3	11.8	8.8
	1970	74.8	75.6	67.0	57.2	47.5	37.9	28.7	20.0	16.0	12.3	9.2
	1980	78.6	78.4	69.7	59.9	50.1	40.5	31.1	22.1	17.9	14.0	10.5
	1987*	79.8	79.6	70.7	61.0	51.2	41.5	32.0	23.0	18.8	14.7	11.1
							F					
Males	1950	62.9	66.2	58.2	48.8	39.7	30.8	22.6	15.4	12.3	9.4	7.0
Hommes	1960	66.9	68.0	59.5	49.9	40.5	31.4	22.9	15.6	12.5	9.6	7.2
	1970	68.4	68.8	60.2	50.7	41.4	32.2	23.7	16.2	13.0	10.2	7.8
	1980	70.2	70.0	61.3	51.8	42.7	33.4	24.8	17.3	14.0	10.9	8.2
	1989*	72.5	72.1	63.3	53.6	44.4	35.2	26.5	18.8	15.4	12.1	9.2
Females	1950	68.5	71.1	63.1	53.5	44.3	35.2	26.5	18.4	14.6	11.3	8.4
Femmes	1960	73.6	74.3	65.7	55.9	46.4	36.9	27.9	19.5	15.6	12.0	8.9
	1970	75.9	76.1	67.4	57.6	48.0	38.5	29.4	20.8	16.8	13.1	9.8
	1980	78.4	78.1	69.3	59.6	49.9	40.3	31.1	22.4	18.2	14.2	10.7
	1989*	80.7	80.2	71.4	61.5	51.8	42.2	32.9	24.0	19.8	15.7	11.9
							IRL					
Males	1950-52	64.5	66.9	58.8	49.3	40.3	31.3	22.8	15.4	12.1	9.2	6.8
Hommes	1960-62	68.1	69.3	60.8	51.1	41.7	32.4	23.5	15.8	12.6	9.7	7.1
	1970-72	68.8	69.2	60.6	51.0	41.5	32.1	23.3	15.6	12.4	9.7	7.3
	1980-82	70.1	69.9	61.3	51.6	42.1	32.6	23.6	15.9	12.6	9.7	7.3
	1989	71.0	71.0	62.0	52.0	43.0	33.0	24.0	16.0	13.0	10.0	7.0
Females	1950-52	67.1	68.8	60.6	51.2	42.2	33.3	24.7	16.8	13.3	10.2	7.6
Femmes	1960-62	71.9	72.7	64.1	54.3	44.7	35.3	26.3	18.1	14.4	11.0	8.1
	1970-72	73.5	73.8	65.1	55.3	45.6	36.0	27.0	18.7	15.0	11.5	8.5
	1980-82	75.6	75.4	66.6	56.8	47.0	37.3	28.0	19.5	15.7	12.2	9.1
	1989	77.0	76.0	67.0	58.0	48.0	38.0	29.0	20.0	16.0	13.0	9.0

Annex 3
Expectation of life at certain ages (years)

T 2

Espérance de vie à certains âges (années)

Sex / Sexe	Year / Année	Age / Âge										
		0	1	10	20	30	40	50	60	65	70	75
I												
Males	1950	63.7	67.3	59.8	50.3	41.1	32.0	23.5	16.0	..	9.6	..
Hommes	1960	67.2	69.4	61.2	51.7	42.3	33.1	24.3	16.7	..	10.4	..
	1970	69.0	70.1	61.6	52.0	42.6	33.2	24.4	16.7	..	10.3	..
	1980	70.6	70.7	62.0	52.4	42.9	33.4	24.5	16.8	13.3	10.3	7.8
	1988*	73.2	73.0	64.1	54.4	45.0	35.4	26.3	18.2	14.7	11.5	8.7
Females	1950	67.2	70.4	62.9	53.3	44.0	34.7	25.8	17.5	..	10.4	..
Femmes	1960	72.3	75.1	65.8	56.1	46.4	37.0	27.8	19.3	..	11.8	..
	1970	74.9	75.8	67.1	57.3	47.6	38.1	28.8	20.2	..	12.4	..
	1980	77.4	77.4	68.6	58.8	49.0	39.4	30.0	21.2	17.1	13.3	9.9
	1988*	79.7	79.4	70.5	60.6	50.8	41.1	31.7	22.7	18.5	14.5	10.9
L												
Males	1949-51	63.4	66.0	57.9	48.7	39.5	30.6	22.4	15.2	12.2	9.5	6.9
Hommes	1961-63	66.5	68.0	59.6	50.0	41.0	31.7	22.9	15.5	12.5	9.8	7.4
	1970-72	67.1	67.7	59.0	49.4	40.2	31.0	22.2	15.2	12.1	9.5	7.4
	1978-80	69.1	68.9	60.2	50.7	41.3	32.0	23.2	15.5	12.3	9.5	7.2
	1985-87	70.6	70.1	61.4	51.9	42.6	33.2	24.2	16.4	13.1	10.1	7.5
Females	1949-51	68.2	70.3	61.9	52.4	43.1	33.9	25.0	16.9	13.3	10.1	7.5
Femmes	1961-63	72.2	73.2	64.7	54.9	45.2	35.7	26.7	18.3	14.5	11.1	8.3
	1970-72	73.4	73.7	65.1	55.3	45.6	36.1	27.1	18.8	14.9	11.5	8.5
	1978-80	75.9	75.7	67.0	57.2	47.5	37.9	28.6	19.9	16.0	12.2	8.8
	1985-87	77.9	77.5	68.6	58.8	49.0	39.4	30.1	21.3	17.2	13.3	9.8
NL												
Males	1950-52	70.6	71.6	63.4	53.7	44.3	34.9	25.9	17.8	14.1	10.9	8.1
Hommes	1960	71.5	71.8	63.4	53.7	44.2	34.7	25.7	17.7	14.2	11.1	8.3
	1970	70.7	70.8	62.3	52.7	43.2	33.7	24.7	16.8	13.6	10.7	8.2
	1981	72.7	72.4	63.7	53.9	44.3	34.8	25.6	17.5	14.0	11.0	8.5
	1989*	73.7	73.2	64.4	54.6	45.0	35.4	26.2	17.9	14.3	11.1	8.4
Females	1950-52	72.9	73.5	65.1	55.4	45.7	36.3	27.1	18.6	14.7	11.3	8.4
Femmes	1960	75.3	75.4	66.9	57.1	47.3	37.7	28.4	19.7	15.7	12.0	8.9
	1970	76.5	76.3	67.7	57.9	48.1	38.5	29.2	20.5	16.5	12.8	9.5
	1981	79.3	78.9	70.1	60.3	50.5	40.8	31.4	22.6	18.5	14.6	11.1
	1989*	79.9	79.4	70.5	60.7	50.9	41.2	31.9	23.0	18.9	14.9	11.4
P												
Males	1950	56.4	61.5	56.3	47.2	38.9	30.6	22.7	15.5	12.3	9.5	..
Hommes	1960	61.2	66.2	59.8	50.3	41.2	32.3	23.8	16.2	13.0	10.1	..
	1970	64.2	67.2	59.4	49.9	40.6	31.6	23.2	15.5	12.2	9.3	..
	1979	67.7	68.7	60.3	50.9	41.7	32.6	24.0	16.3	12.9	9.8	..
	1989*	70.9	71.0	62.4	52.9	43.8	34.7	25.9	18.0	14.5	11.3	8.5
Females	1950	61.6	66.3	61.3	52.1	43.5	34.8	26.2	18.0	14.4	11.0	..
Femmes	1960	66.9	71.4	65.0	55.4	45.9	36.6	27.6	19.1	15.3	11.8	..
	1970	70.8	73.4	65.4	55.7	46.1	36.7	27.5	18.9	15.0	11.4	..
	1979	75.2	76.0	67.5	57.8	48.1	38.5	29.3	20.6	16.5	12.8	..
	1989*	77.9	77.9	69.2	59.5	49.7	40.2	30.9	22.0	17.8	13.8	10.3

| Expectation of life at certain ages (years) | | T 2 | | | | | Espérance de vie à certains âges (années) | | | | |

Sex Sexe	Year Année	Age Âge										
		0	1	10	20	30	40	50	60	65	70	75
							UK					
Males Hommes	1950	66.2	67.5	59.1	49.5	40.2	30.9	22.2	14.8	11.7	9.0	6.7
	1960	67.9	68.7	60.1	50.4	40.9	31.5	22.6	15.0	11.9	9.3	7.1
	1970	68.7	69.1	60.5	50.8	41.3	31.8	22.9	15.2	12.0	9.4	7.2
	1980	70.2	70.2	61.4	51.8	42.2	32.7	23.7	15.9	12.6	9.7	7.4
	1988	72.2	71.9	63.1	53.4	43.8	34.3	25.1	17.0	13.6	10.6	8.2
Females Femmes	1950	71.2	72.1	63.6	53.9	44.4	35.1	26.2	17.9	14.2	10.9	8.0
	1960	73.7	74.2	65.5	55.7	46.0	36.4	27.3	18.9	15.1	11.6	8.7
	1970	75.0	75.2	66.5	56.6	46.9	37.3	28.2	19.8	16.0	12.4	9.4
	1980	76.2	76.1	67.3	57.5	47.7	38.1	28.9	20.4	16.6	13.0	9.8
	1988	77.9	77.5	68.7	58.8	49.0	39.3	30.0	21.3	17.5	13.9	10.7

Expectation of life at 60 years - 1989
Espérance de vie à 60 ans - 1989

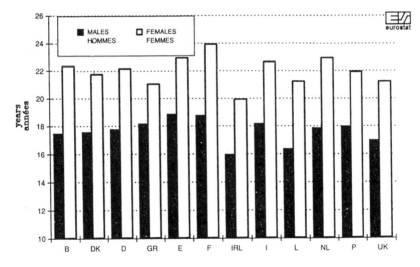

Annex 3

Sex ratio 1.1.1990 - EUR 12
Rapport de masculinité 1.1.1990 - EUR 12

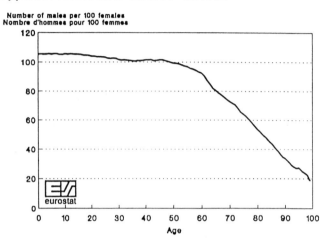

165

T 3 **Proportion of women in the age group 65 and over, by Member States, at 1 January 1989** ; (in per cent) 1

	65-69	70-74	75-79	80-84	85-89	90-94	≥ 95	≥ 60	≥ 80
B	55	58	63	68	72	76	76	58	70
DK	54	56	59	65	69	72	76	57	67
D	62	64	67	70	73	79	81	63	72
E	55	59	61	64	67	71	74	57	66
F	55	58	62	67	72	79	83	59	70
GR	54	56	57	59	61	60	66	55	60
IRL	53	55	57	62	67	73	80	56	65
I	56	58	61	65	70	74	80	58	67
LUX	60	59	64	69	72	80	100	61	71
NL	55	58	62	69	71	73	72	58	69
P	55	57	60	65	69	73	76	58	67
UK	54	58	61	67	74	79	84	58	70
EUR 12	56	59	62	67	71	76	80	59	69

Source : EUROSTAT, 1991 ; based upon tables B-2, B-7, B-9.

1 100 % = total number of persons in the age group.

Annex 3

T 4   **Population aged 75 and over in the countries of the European Community, by sex and marital status, 1981-82** (percentages add across the table)

	single	m a l e married	widowed	divorced	single	f e m a l e married	widowed	divorced
B	7	57	35	1	10	20	68	2
DK	8	58	31	3	14	20	61	5
D	4	66	29	1	11	17	70	2
E	7	61	31	1	14	19	66	1
F	7	63	28	2	10	20	68	2
GR	4	73	22	1	4	28	67	1
IRE	25	47	28	- [1]	25	15	60	-
I	6	64	30	0 [2]	13	19	68	0
LUX	10	57	33	0	14	17	68	1
NL	6	61	32	1	12	23	64	1
P	6	63	30	1	13	23	63	1
UK	8	61	30	1	15	20	64	1
EUR 12	6	63	30	1	12	20	67	1

Source : EUROSTAT : Censuses of the population in the Community countries, 1981-1982, Luxemburg, 1988, calculations by author.

[1] None.
[2] Less than 0,5 %.

T 5 **Population aged 75 and over in the countries of the European Community, by sex, age and marital status, 1981-82 ;** (percentages add across the table)

	N x 1000 = 100 %	male single	married	widowed	divorced	N x 1000 = 100 %	female single	married	widowed	divorced
EUR 12										
75-79	3 377	7	70	22	1	5 533	12	27	59	2
80-84	1 665	6	58	35	1	3 362	12	15	71	2
≥ 85	777	6	41	52	1	2 066	13	7	79	1
B										
75-79	111	7	65	26	2	188	9	28	61	2
80-84	57	7	51	41	1	116	10	16	73	1
≥ 85	28	6	34	59	1	67	12	7	80	1
DK										
75-79	59	8	66	22	4	88	14	28	54	5
80-84	33	7	56	34	3	57	14	17	64	5
≥ 85	19	6	38	54	2	38	15	7	74	4
D										
75-79	743	4	73	22	1	1 308	11	23	64	2
80-84	348	4	59	36	1	734	12	12	74	2
≥ 85	136	4	44	51	1	383	12	5	81	2
E										
75-79	336	8	68	23	1	516	14	26	59	1
80-84	164	7	55	37	1	299	14	15	71	0
≥ 85	82	7	39	54	0	182	14	7	79	0
F										
75-79	615	7	70	21	2	1 009	9	29	59	3
80-84	331	7	60	32	1	677	10	16	71	3
≥ 85	149	5	43	51	1	470	11	6	81	2

Annex 3

T 5 : continued

	N x 1000 = 100 %	m a l e				N x 1000 = 100 %	f e m a l e			
		single	married	widowed	divorced		single	married	widowed	divorced
GR										
75-79	107	3	79	17	1	135	4	36	59	1
80-84	55	3	71	25	1	82	4	24	71	1
≥ 85	29	5	58	37	0	47	4	16	80	0
IRE										
75-79	29	25	53	22	-	39	25	20	55	-
80-84	15	25	44	31	-	25	24	12	64	-
≥ 85	8	23	34	43	-	15	24	7	69	-
I										
75-79	559	6	71	22	2	878	13	26	61	0
80-84	276	6	58	36	0	525	13	15	72	0
≥ 85	133	5	41	54	0	312	13	7	80	0
LUX										
75-79	4	11	64	25	0	6	13	23	63	1
80-84	2	9	53	37	1	4	15	12	72	1
≥ 85	1	10	33	57	0	2	13	5	81	1
NL										
75-79	126	6	71	22	1	202	11	32	55	2
80-84	71	6	58	35	1	128	11	19	69	1
≥ 85	44	6	37	56	1	79	12	10	77	1
P										
75-79	82	6	69	24	1	135	13	31	55	1.
80-84	37	5	57	37	1	73	13	18	68	1
≥ 85	16	6	41	52	1	41	13	9	77	1
UK										
75-79	608	8	68	23	1	1 027	14	28	57	1
80-84	277	8	55	36	1	642	15	16	68	1
≥ 85	133	7	39	53	1	431	16	7	76	1

Source : EUROSTAT : Censuses of the population in the Community countries, 1981-1982, Luxemburg, 1988, calculations by author.

T 5 : continued

	N x 1000 = 100 %	m a l e				N x 1000 = 100 %	f e m a l e			
		single	married	widowed	divorced		single	married	widowed	divorced
GR										
75-79	107	3	79	17	1	135	4	36	59	1
80-84	55	3	71	25	1	82	4	24	71	1
≥ 85	29	5	58	37	0	47	4	16	80	0
IRE										
75-79	29	25	53	22	-	39	25	20	55	-
80-84	15	25	44	31	-	25	24	12	64	-
≥ 85	8	23	34	43	-	15	24	7	69	-
I										
75-79	559	6	71	22	2	878	13	26	61	0
80-84	276	6	58	36	0	525	13	15	72	0
≥ 85	133	5	41	54	0	312	13	7	80	0
LUX										
75-79	4	11	64	25	0	6	13	23	63	1
80-84	2	9	53	37	1	4	15	12	72	1
≥ 85	1	10	33	57	0	2	13	5	81	1
NL										
75-79	126	6	71	22	1	202	11	32	55	2
80-84	71	6	58	35	1	128	11	19	69	1
≥ 85	44	6	37	56	1	79	12	10	77	1
P										
75-79	82	6	69	24	1	135	13	31	55	1
80-84	37	5	57	37	1	73	13	18	68	1
≥ 85	16	6	41	52	1	41	13	9	77	1
UK										
75-79	608	8	68	23	1	1 027	14	28	57	1
80-84	277	8	55	36	1	642	15	16	68	1
≥ 85	133	7	39	53	1	431	16	7	76	1

Source : EUROSTAT : Censuses of the population in the Community countries, 1981-1982, Luxemburg, 1988, calculations by author.

Annex 3

T 6   **Difficulties in activities of daily living among people living at home ; proportions among age groups specified in certain Member States** ; as a percentage of the age-group concerned

		feeding self	washing self	Difficulties with taking bath or shower	dressing self	cutting toenails	picking up something from the floor
B	1985						
	≥ 75 years	10-1-1 [1]	15-5-2	12-15-16	19-6-2	•	•
D [2]	1991		*to wash/ take a shower*	*bath*			
	≥ 70 years	3-1 [3]	9-6	11-14	8-5	•	•
DK	1988						
	70-79 years	•		5-6 [3]	7-3	10-25	•
	≥ 80 years	•		16-12	19-4	14-52	•
F	1990 [4]						
	≥ 60 years	3	11	•	10	•	36
	1992 [5]	2	8	•	7	•	17
I [6]	1982/87/89 [7]						
	75-79 years	4	•	29	10	34	20
	80-84 years	7	•	51	18	54	30
	≥ 85 years	6	•	60	21	65	41
IRE [8] about 1981							
	70-79 years	•	•	25-39 [9]	12-18	•	•
	≥ 80 years	•	•	55-72	27-40	•	•
NL [10] 1982							
	65-74 years	•	4	•	6	•	•
	≥ 75 years	•	4-12 [11]	•	5-13	•	•
P	1987 [12]						
	75-84 years	7	•	•	20	•	•
	≥ 85 years	18	•	•	37	•	•
UK	1980 [13]						
	≥ 65 years	1-1-0 [1]		10-7-1	•	15-27	•

[1] The first figure shows the proportion *able to do it but with difficulty* ; the second is the proportion *unable to do it without help* ; and the third figure is the proportion *unable to perform the activity*.

[2] Includes the former *East Germany*.

[3] The first figure shows the proportion *able to perform the activity without help, but with difficulty* ; the second figure represents the proportion *unable to do it without help, or not at all*.

[4] National survey, representative of these receiving home/domestic help in rural areas, i.e. a population characterised by need for domestic help [Jani-Le Bris, 1990].

T 6 : continued

		getting in/ out of bed	going to the toilet	Difficulties with moving about indoors	outdoors	walking ... metres	climbing stairs
B	1985 ≥ 75 years	19-3-1 [1]	14-1-1	16-1-2	12-16-13	•	16-1-2
D [2]	1991 ≥ 70 years	5-3 [3]	•	9-3	•	•	34-8
DK	1988 70-79 years	•	•	10-1 [1]	15-4	*400 m* 46 [14]	23-7
	≥ 80 years	•	•	24-3	22-20		34-20
F	1990 [4] ≥ 60 years	12	•	12	21	•	42
	1992 [5] ≥ 80 years	7	•	7	18	•	23
I [6]	1982/87/89 [7] 75-79 years	8	9	7	•	*400 m* 32	17
	80-84 years	15	17	14	•	45	31
	≥ 85 years	17	19	17	•	52	41
IRE [8]	about 1981 70-79 years	•	•	•	•	*800 m* 26-45 [9]	36-48
	≥ 80 years	•	•	•	•	60-74	64-76
NL [10]	1982 65-74 years	•	•	•	•	•	13-17 [11]
	≥ 75 years	•	•	•	•	•	22-28
P	1987 [12] 65-74 years	•	•	•	•	*50 m* 32-2 [3]	49-5-4 [1]
	≥ 75 years	•	•	•	•	48-7	52-13-11
UK	1980 [13] ≥ 65 years	•	•	7-1-1 [1]	10-5-7	•	21-4-4

[5] National survey, representative of people affiliated to a middle managers' fund, meaning that the population involved is more privileged socio-economically than the French average. [Jani-Le Bris, Luquet, 1992].

[6] Regional survey, Northern Italy. The proportions refer to numbers *completely dependant for help*.

[7] Accumulated figures from three years.

[8] Based upon O'Shea, 1991, p. 67.

[9] The first proportion relates to men, the second to women.

[10] Source : ibid., note 8, p. 156.

[11] The first proportion relates to men, the second to women.

[12] Combined categories of *only with help* and *with some help*.

[13] Based upon Evandrou, 1990.

[14] Unable to walk 400 metres : 1986/87

Annex 3

T 7   **Interviewee's assessment of their health ; Spain and Italy ;**
      as a proportion of the age group specified

		good / very good	moderate	poor / very poor	total
E	1989				
	70-74 years	24	50	26	100
	75-79 years	22	50	28	100
	80-84 years	20	52	28	100
	≥ 85 years	20	45	35	100
I	1986 [1]				
	≥ 75 years				
	men	39	•	59	100 [2]
	women	41	•	59	100 [3]

---

[1] Based upon Espace Social Européen, 1991 : 139

[2] The total is less than 100 % since the 2 % who did not reply are not included.

[3] Although women's non-response was also 2 %, the total is nevertheless 100 % since the original source contains an error.

T 8   **Indications concerning mental deterioration** [1] **for some Member States ;**
as a proportion of the age group specified

B	≥ 75 years	senile dementia	14 %	estimated
		depressive state	23 %	population at home ; 1985
		loss of memory	9 %	
		disorientation in space or time	29 %	population living in institutions ; 1984
D	≥ 65 years	mental illnesses	25 %	partial surveys ; year : ?
	≥ 75 years	dementia syndrome		
		75-79 years	10-12 %	
		80-90 years	20-24 %	
		> 90 years	> 30 %	
		Most are living at home in the community		
DK	≥ 65 years	senile dementia the risk increases exponentially with age	4-6 %	1990
	≥ 70 years	depression	6 %	1988
		Most are living at home in the community		
F	≥ 75 years	mental deterioration		1982
		75-84 years	4 %	
		≥ 85 years	14 %	
		Most are living at home in the community		
I	≥ 65 years	mental deficiencies		[Espace Social Européen, 1991 : 128]
		65-74 ans	3 %	
		≥ 75 ans	11 %	
IRE	age : ?	neurological problems	12 %	[ibid. : 119] year : ?
NL	≥ 65 years	some form of dementia	1-6 %	estimations, 1990
		depression	15-30 %	

---

[1] The terms employed by the authors, or their translators, have been used.

Annex 3

T 9 **Classification of disability, population living at home ;** proportions of age groups specified.

		± without disability	slight or moderate disability	severe disability	total	disability/ dysfunction [1]	handi- cap [1]
B	1985						
	≥ 65 years	73	11	16	100		
	≥ 75 years	60	16	24	100		
D	year : ?						
	65-79 years	88	9	3	100		
	≥ 80 years	47	37	16	100		
E	1987/88						
	75-79 years					22	22
	80-84 years					33	18
	≥ 80 years					50	26
F	1980/81						
	≥ 70 years	56	38	6	100		
	≥ 80 years	38	50	12	100		
IRE	1990 ?						
	age : ?	46			[O'Shea, 1991 : 13 ; 69]		
P	1989						
	≥ 65 years			8 [2]			
UK	1980						
	75-79 years	68	25	7	100		
	≥ 80 years	46	31	22	100		

[1] Not defined.

[2] Proportion of age group 65 and over receiving supplementary benefit for major disability; no indication of residence.

T 10   Expectation of life (E.L.) and expectation of life without
disability (E.L.W.D.), by sex and age, France, 1982

age	E.L. years			E.L.W.D. years			E.L.W.D./E.L. %	
	m	f	f-m	m	f	f-m	m	f
0	70,7	78,9	8,2	61,9	67,1	5,2	87,4	85,0
5	66,6	74,6	8,0	57,8	62,8	5,0	86,6	84,2
10	61,7	69,7	8,0	53,1	58,0	4,9	85,9	83,2
15	56,8	64,8	8,0	48,3	53,2	4,9	85,0	82,1
20	52,2	60,0	7,8	43,8	48,5	4,7	83,9	80,8
25	47,6	55,1	7,5	39,4	43,8	4,4	82,8	79,5
30	43,0	50,3	7,3	35,0	39,2	4,2	81,4	77,9
35	38,3	45,5	7,2	30,6	34,6	4,0	79,6	76,0
40	33,7	40,7	7,0	26,2	30,0	3,8	77,7	73,7
45	29,3	36,0	6,7	22,2	25,5	3,3	75,4	70,1
50	25,1	31,4	6,3	18,3	21,2	2,9	72,5	67,5
55	21,3	27,0	5,7	14,9	17,1	2,2	70,0	63,3
60	17,6	22,7	5,1	11,7	13,3	1,6	66,5	58,6
65	14,3	18,5	4,2	9,1	9,9	0,8	63,6	53,5
70	11,2	14,5	3,3	6,5	6,9	0,4	58,0	47,6
75	8,5	10,9	2,4	4,4	4,3	— 0,1	51,8	39,4
80	6,2	7,9	1,7	2,8	2,4	— 0,4	45,2	30,4
85	4,5	5,5	1,0	1,5	1,5	0	33,3	27,3

Source : COLVEZ A., ROBINE J.M.: L'espérance de vie sans incapacité
en France en 1982, in Population, n° 6, novembre/décembre
1986, Editions de l'INED, Paris, p 1033

Annex 3

T 11 **Indicators of mobility, by age and sex ; Portugal, Ireland, Denmark ;**
as a proportion of the group

P 1987	65-74		75-84		≥ 85	
	M	W	M	W	M	W
walking 50 m. on level surface [1]	22	35	33	45	28	48
climbing stairs [2]	51	67	69	82	87	90

IRE [3] 1982	65-69		70-79		≥ 80	
	M	W	M	W	M	W
taking the bus [4]	37	40	41	61	67	82
walking ≥ 800 m [4]	23	26	26	45	60	74
climbing stairs [4]	28	30	36	48	64	76

DK [5] 1989	70-79		≥ 80	
	M	W	M	W
confined to home	5	10	17	32
can go out, but with difficulty	11	9	10	17
can go out without difficulty	82	79	72	50

[1] Combined responses : with difficulty — only with help — unable.
[2] Combined responses : with difficulty — only with help. (Unable not categorised.)
[3] Based upon Espace Social European, 1991 : 119
[4] Difficulties (without further precision).
[5] As the criteria are mutually exclusive, each column stands for 100 % minus x % confined to their beds or armchairs.

T 12 **Older persons living in institutions** [1] ; as a proportion of various age groups

	≥ 65 years[2]	≥ 75 years	≥ 85 years	≥ 90 years
B	4	13		
D	5		17 [3]	21 [3]
DK	7			46 [4]
E	2		6 [5]	
F	6	10 [6]	20 [6]	25 [6]
GR	1			
I	2			
IRE	5			
LUX				
NL	10		47	
P	2	4	7	
UK	5	9		

[1] The definitions are not identical either for all the countries or all the age groups. The both include and exclude people living in a hospital, residential homes and private profit-making homes.
[2] Source : Nijkamp, 1991 : 46, T 8
[3] Source : KDA, 1991 : 5. Estimated from 1987 census.
[4] All types of communal residence.
[5] Source : Perez Ortis, 1991 : 21
[6] 1982 census.

CARERS' CHARTER

1. Carers have the right to be recognised for the central role which they play in community care and in creating a community of caring.

2. Carers have the right to acknowledge and address their own needs for personal fulfilment.

3. Carers have the right to acknowledge and address their own needs in relation to their contribution to their family and community.

4. Carers have the right to practical help in carrying out the tasks of caregiving, including domestic help, home adaptations, appliances, incontinence services and help with transport.

5. Carers have the right to support services, e.g. public health nurses, day centres and home helps in providing medical, personal and domestic care.

6. Care have the right to respite care both for short spells as in day hospitals and for longer periods to enable them to have time for themselves.

7. Carers have the right to emotional and financial support.

8. Carers have the right to financial support and recompense which does not preclude carers taking employment or in sharing care with other people.

9. Carers have the right to regular assessment and review of their needs and those of the people for whom they care.

10. Carers have the right to easy access to information and advice.

Annex 4

11. Carers have the right to expect involvement of all family members.

12. Carers have the right to have counselling made available to them at different stages of the caring process including bereavement counselling.

13. Carers have the right to skills' training and development of their potential.

14. Carers have the right to expect their families, public authorities and community members to provide a plan for services and support for carers, taking into account the unique demographic developments up to and beyond the year 2000.

15. Carers have the right to involvement at all levels of policy planning, to participate and contribute to the planning of an integrated and co-ordinated service for carers.

16. Carers have the right to have an infrastructure of care, a supportive network to which they can relate when the need arises.

Do you look after someone physically or mentally disabled, frail or ill, at home?

Whether you are caring for your husband or wife, partner, parent or child, relative or friend,

make sure you're getting the services and financial benefits you are entitled to.

RING US ON : 081 314 5897

CARERS LEWISHAM,

21 Slagrove Place,
SE13 7XW

(24 hour ansaphone
outside office hours)

Coping at home - day-to-day help

COMMUNITY CARE TEAMS

Lewisham Social Services can help you, as a carer, to look after the person you care for. For example:

* someone to help a person get washed and dressed

* meals on wheels and help with housework and shopping

* sitting service

* day care (one or more days a week at a day centre)

* respite care (a break) - ie care for your relative with a family or in a residential home while you have a break of up to 1 or 2 weeks.

* aids and adaptations (from the O.T. or 'Rehab' team) eg. grab rails, ramp, bath aids, a special chair.

Ring **081 695 6000** and ask for the **Community Care Officer** for your road. You have a right to ask the Community Care service for an assessment of your and your relative's needs. Someone will visit you and talk through how best to help.

CROSSROADS CARE ATTENDANT SCHEME

Crossroads is a voluntary agency based at 23 Slagrove Place, SE13. Tel. **081 314 1445.**

Crossroads arranges for a trained care attendant to look after the person you care for at home for 2 hours or more each week. You can use this time just as you choose eg going out or doing something at home.

This is a free service and offers carers the chance of a regular break. Crossroads has proved to be a very popular resource to carers - so unfortunately service is limited.

VOLUNTARY CARE CENTRE

The Voluntary Care Centre is a voluntary agency based at 55 b, Dartmouth Rd, SE23. Tel. **081 291 1747.**

They can help carers in the Sydenham/Forest Hill area, with practical tasks, befriending, sitting with relatives.

Health Care

Your GP can advise you on health services - remember YOUR health is important as well as the person you care for.

You can phone or call in yourself to your local Health Centre, and ask for a **District Nurse** to visit you . She or he can arrange regular nursing care at home for someone who needs help, and can also advise on lifting techniques, diet and coping with incontinence.

Ask at your Health Centre also about physiotherapy, dental care and chiropody.

HEALTH CENTRES	
Central Lewisham Health Centre, 410 Lewisham High St.	690 9723
Honor Oak Health Centre, 20 Turnham Rd, SE4	639 8811
Jenner Health Centre, 201 Stanstead Rd SE23	690 2231
Lee Health Centre, 2 Handen Rd, SE12	318 4431
South Lewisham Centre, 50 Connisborough Cresc. SE6	698 8921
Downham Health Centre, 24 Churchdown, SE26	695 6644
Sydenham Green Health Centre, 26 Holmshaw Close SE26	778 1333
Waldron Health Centre, Stanley St SE8	691 4621

Looking after you, the carer

Caring is often very physically tiring. And also, however much you may want to care for someone, it can be emotionally exhausting too. So, carers often need more than just practical help.

You may be feeling very much alone. You may have mixed feelings of guilt, sadness, frustration, resentment, anxiety. It is often a surprise and a relief for a carer to find that other carers have had similar feelings, and that talking to someone, and being LISTENED to, really can help.

There are carers support groups now at nearly all the health centres. We can put you in touch with one.

Or, you may feel you want time just to talk with one person.

Some people who could offer you time to talk about how you feel:

* **Carers Lewisham** ..... 081 314 5897 (you can also ring us if you're a former carer)*
* **Contact a Family** .... 081 857 9169 (if you care for a child with special needs)
* **Samaritans** (24hr.no) 081 692 5228
* **Women's Advice & Counselling Service** at the Albany Centre 081 692 6268

Annex 5

Cash Help

Many people are entitled to benefits they do not claim. These are some you need to know about:

ATTENDANCE ALLOWANCE

If someone needs help with personal care eg washing or going to the toilet, or is unsafe left alone for long because they're confused or frail (and if they have needed looking after for 6 months or longer, or are terminally ill) - they are entitled to this benefit.

Claim Attendance Allowance in the name of the person cared for - no questions are asked about income or savings, just about how much help they need.

Ask for leaflet NI 205 - from post office or DSS

INVALID CARE ALLOWANCE

This is an allowance for YOU the carer. You can claim if you are under 65, and cannot work full time because you look after someone.(You can earn up to £20 per week).

The person you care for must receive (or have applied for) Attendance Allowance, and need 35 hours care a week.

You will be asked about other benefits you or your partner receives as some exclude people from ICA (but it IS worth applying). ICA also protects your pension rights.

If your receive Income Support, Rent Rebate or Poll Tax Rebate, claiming ICA entitles you to a £10 'Carer's Premium' on one of these. Ask for leaflet NI 212 from the DSS office.

INDEPENDENT LIVING FUND

This is a special fund to enable a frail or disabled person to live at home - single grants or regular payments can be made to help the carer cope eg by being able to pay for regular relief care at home while you get a break. The person cared for must be over 16, and receiving the higher rate of Attendance Allowance.

Each person is assessed for their individual needs. Contact Carers Lewisham for details or application forms.

WHO TO CONTACT FOR FINANCIAL ADVICE, OR HELP FILLING IN FORMS

* Carers Lewisham - ring us on 081 314 5897

* Your local library can tell you of your nearest advice agency.

* Citizen' Advice Bureaux (see phone book). Home visits may be possible.

LOCAL DSS (DEPT. OF SOCIAL SECURITY) OFFICES

SE26 area:	6 Cargreen Rd SE25	653 8822
SE4,SE8,SE14,SE10:	110 Norman Rd SE10	858 8070
SE6,SE13,SE23:	9 Rushey Green SE6	698 6144
SE12:	62 Well Hall Rd SE9	850 2102
SE3:	48 Woolwich New Rd SE18.	854 2275
Bromley:	1 Westmoreland Rd, Bromley.	460 9911

TEL: (081) 314 5897

CARERS GROUPS IN LEWISHAM

WHAT ARE CARERS GROUPS?

The groups meet regularly, and provide a relaxed and friendly place for carers to meet with each other; people in a carers group will understand your practical difficulties and mixed feelings.

Sometimes speakers are invited on topics of interest to carers in the group - which could range from welfare rights to local history, relaxation to jewellery making. Often, there are socials or outings.

If transport is a problem or you need to arrange a sitter for the person you look after, we'll try to help.

HOW CAN A GROUP HELP ME?

Someone to talk to
Information on how to cope more easily.
A chance to meet new people

HOW DO I FIND A CARERS GROUP?

There are now carers groups at nearly every health centre in the borough. They meet during the day and on different days of the week. So you could either choose the group nearest to you or one on a day that suits you.

The groups are open to all carers, who ever they care for.

Also, there are carers groups to meet special needs or interests - including a group for black and ethnic minority carers, and a group for carers who are at work during the day. Both these groups meet in the evening.

CARERS DROP IN

at: Telegraph Hill Community
    Centre, Kitto Road, SE14
on: Mondays, weekly,
    1.30 - 3.30 pm
Contact: Evelyn Sterling
         639 0865/639 0214

JENNER HEALTH CENTRE

at: Jenner Health Centre,
    201 Stanstead Road, SE6
on: Tuesdays, fortnightly,
    2 - 4 pm

CENTRAL LEWISHAM CARERS GROUP

at: C. Lewisham Clinic,
    410 Lewisham High Street,
    SE13
on: Tuesdays, fortnightly,
    2 - 4 pm
Contact: Alison Newbegin:
          690 9723 (office hours)

WELLS PARK CARERS GROUP

at: 106 Wells Park Road, SE26
on: Wednesdays, fortnightly,
    1.30 - 3.30 pm
Contact: Amanda 291 3332
          (office hours)
    or: Cyril 778 7458 (eves)

SOUTH LEWISHAM CARERS GROUP

at: S. Lewisham Health Centre,
    Conisborough Crescent, SE6
on: Wednesdays, fortnightly,
    12 - 2.15 pm

Annex 5

DOWNHAM CARERS GROUP

at: Downham Clinic,
    24 Churchdown, Bromley.
on: Tuesdays, fortnightly,
    1.30-3.30 pm

SYDENHAM CARERS GROUPS

at: Sydenham Health Centre,
    26 Holmshaw Close, SE26
on: Wednesdays, fortnightly,
    1.30-3.30 pm
Contact: Lois Lennon: 778 4740

DEPTFORD/NEW CROSS CARERS

New group starting soon.
Contact: Julie, Carers Lewisham
         314 5897

LEE GROUP

For details: Contact Linda,
Carers Lewisham, 314 5897

CARERS OF PEOPLE WITH STROKES

at: Grove Hill Court,
    Hildenburgh Gardens, Downham
on: Wednesdays, fortnightly,
    7 - 8 pm
Contact: James Davies 698 6333

BLACK CARERS SUPPORT GROUP

Meets 6-weekly at alternate
places:

at: Ladywell Baths,
    261 Lewisham High St. SE13
or: CROSSROADS office
    Peter Pan Block,
    23 Slagrove Place, SE13

on: Wednesdays, 7 - 9 pm
    Mondays,   1 - 3 pm

WORKING CARERS

We are planning to hold an
evening session once a month,
where carers who are at work
during the day, can drop in for
advice and information on
services and benefits.
Contact: Carers Lewisham for more
         details.

FORMER CARERS GROUP

at: Ballantyne,
    Lushington Rd. SE6
on: Mondays, monthly, 2 pm

CARERS OF PEOPLE WITH DEMENTIA

at: Ladywell EMI Day Centre,
    25 Slagrove Place, SE13
on: Wednesdays, fortnightly,
    1.30 - 3.30 pm

Contact: Brian Walker
          690 5244 (office hrs.)

CARERS OF PEOPLE WITH LEARNING DIFFICULTIES:

at: Mulberry Day Centre
    15, Amersham Vale, SE14.
    691 4515

Parents and carers coffee
mornings:
on: Wednesday, fortnightly,
    10 - 12 pm

Also contact: Joan McCleod, Team
for People with Learning
Difficulties : **695 6000**
to find out about short term
groups.

RELATIVES OF PEOPLE WITH mental health problems.

*Southbrook Relatives Group

at: Southbrook Advice Centre
    1 Southbrook Rd. SE12
on: Mondays, fortnightly
    4.30 - 5.30 pm
Contact: Joanna Wilkinson or
          Teresa Jenkins 314 1339

*A group has been meeting weekly
at: **Louise House**

To find out more about future
groups for relatives

Contact: Rosemary Wilson
          699 0111 ext. 262

Also contact: Bill Graham at
Independents Day Centre: 852 7489
if interested in a support group
meeting at the Centre.

Where the carers groups have a
contact person listed, you can
ring them direct.   Otherwise,
just phone or write to **Linda** or
Julie -
CARERS LEWISHAM,
21 Slagrove Place, SE13 7XW
Tel: 081 314 5897

Reg. Charity No. 246329   MAY 1991

European Foundation for the Improvement of Living and Working Conditions

Family Care of Dependent Older People in the European Community

Luxembourg: Office for Official Publications of the European Communities, 1993

1993 – 200 p. – 16 x 23.4 cm

ISBN 92-826-6355-8

Price (excluding VAT) in Luxembourg: ECU 20

Venta y suscripciones • Salg og abonnement • Verkauf und Abonnement • Πωλήσεις και συνδρομές
Sales and subscriptions • Vente et abonnements • Vendita e abbonamenti
Verkoop en abonnementen • Venda e assinaturas

BELGIQUE / BELGIË

**Moniteur belge /
Belgisch Staatsblad**

Rue de Louvain 42 / Leuvenseweg 42
B-1000 Bruxelles / B-1000 Brussel
Tél. (02) 512 00 26
Fax (02) 511 01 84

Autres distributeurs /
Overige verkooppunten

**Librairie européenne /
Europese boekhandel**

Rue de la Loi 244 / Wetstraat 244
B-1040 Bruxelles / B-1040 Brussel
Tél. (02) 231 04 35
Fax (02) 735 08 60

Jean de Lannoy

Avenue du Roi 202 / Koningslaan 202
B-1060 Bruxelles / B-1060 Brussel
Tél. (02) 538 51 69
Télex 63220 UNBOOK B
Fax (02) 538 08 41

Document delivery:

Credoc

Rue de la Montagne 34 / Bergstraat 34
Bte 11 / Bus 11
B-1000 Bruxelles / B-1000 Brussel
Tél. (02) 511 69 41
Fax (02) 513 31 95

DANMARK

J. H. Schultz Information A/S

Herstedvang 10-12
DK-2620 Albertslund
Tlf. 43 63 23 00
Fax (Sales) 43 63 19 69
Fax (Management) 43 63 19 49

DEUTSCHLAND

Bundesanzeiger Verlag

Breite Straße 78-80
Postfach 10 05 34
D-50445 Köln
Tel. (02 21) 20 29-0
Telex ANZEIGER BONN 8 882 595
Fax 2 02 92 78

GREECE/ΕΛΛΑΔΑ

G.C. Eleftheroudakis SA

International Bookstore
Nikis Street 4
GR-10563 Athens
Tel. (01) 322 63 23
Telex 219410 ELEF
Fax 323 98 21

ESPAÑA

Boletín Oficial del Estado

Trafalgar, 29
E-28071 Madrid
Tel. (91) 538 22 95
Fax (91) 538 23 49

Mundi-Prensa Libros, SA

Castelló, 37
E-28001 Madrid
Tel. (91) 431 33 99 (Libros)
         431 32 22 (Suscripciones)
         435 36 37 (Dirección)
Télex 49370-MPLI-E
Fax (91) 575 39 98

Sucursal:

Librería Internacional AEDOS

Consejo de Ciento, 391
E-08009 Barcelona
Tel. (93) 488 34 92
Fax (93) 487 76 59

**Llibreria de la Generalitat
de Catalunya**

Rambla dels Estudis, 118 (Palau Moja)
E-08002 Barcelona
Tel. (93) 302 68 35
         302 64 62
Fax (93) 302 12 99

FRANCE

**Journal officiel
Service des publications
des Communautés européennes**

26, rue Desaix
F-75727 Paris Cedex 15
Tél. (1) 40 58 75 00
Fax (1) 40 58 77 00

IRELAND

Government Supplies Agency

4-5 Harcourt Road
Dublin 2
Tel. (1) 66 13 111
Fax (1) 47 80 645

ITALIA

Licosa SpA

Via Duca di Calabria, 1/1
Casella postale 552
I-50125 Firenze
Tel. (055) 64 54 15
Fax 64 12 57
Telex 570466 LICOSA I

GRAND-DUCHÉ DE LUXEMBOURG

Messageries du livre

5, rue Raiffeisen
L-2411 Luxembourg
Tél. 40 10 20
Fax 40 10 24 01

NEDERLAND

SDU Overheidsinformatie

Externe Fondsen
Postbus 20014
2500 EA's-Gravenhage
Tel. (070) 37 89 911
Fax (070) 34 75 778

PORTUGAL

Imprensa Nacional

Casa da Moeda, EP
Rua D. Francisco Manuel de Melo, 5
P-1092 Lisboa Codex
Tel. (01) 69 34 14

**Distribuidora de Livros
Bertrand, Ld.ª**

Grupo Bertrand, SA

Rua das Terras dos Vales, 4-A
Apartado 37
P-2700 Amadora Codex
Tel. (01) 49 59 050
Telex 15798 BERDIS
Fax 49 60 255

UNITED KINGDOM

HMSO Books (Agency section)

HMSO Publications Centre
51 Nine Elms Lane
London SW8 5DR
Tel. (071) 873 9090
Fax 873 8463
Telex 29 71 138

ÖSTERREICH

**Manz'sche Verlags-
und Universitätsbuchhandlung**

Kohlmarkt 16
A-1014 Wien
Tel. (0222) 531 61-133
Telex 112 500 BOX A
Fax (0222) 531 61-181

SUOMI/FINLAND

Akateeminen Kirjakauppa

Keskuskatu 1
PO Box 128
SF-00101 Helsinki
Tel. (0) 121 41
Fax (0) 121 44 41

NORGE

Narvesen Info Center

Bertrand Narvesens vei 2
PO Box 6125 Etterstad
N-0602 Oslo 6
Tel. (22) 57 33 00
Telex 79668 NIC N
Fax (22) 68 19 01

SVERIGE

BTJ AB

Traktorvägen 13
S-22100 Lund
Tel. (046) 18 00 00
Fax (046) 18 01 25
         30 79 47

SCHWEIZ / SUISSE / SVIZZERA

OSEC

Stampfenbachstraße 85
CH-8035 Zürich
Tel. (01) 365 54 49
Fax (01) 365 54 11

ČESKÁ REPUBLIKA

NIS ČR

Havelkova 22
130 00 Praha 3
Tel. (2) 235 84 46
Fax (2) 235 97 88

MAGYARORSZÁG

Euro-Info-Service

Club Sziget
Margitsziget
1138 Budapest
Tel./Fax 1 111 60 61
               1 111 62 16

POLSKA

Business Foundation

ul. Krucza 38/42
00-512 Warszawa
Tel. (22) 21 99 93, 628-28 82
International Fax & Phone
(0-39) 12-00-77

ROMÂNIA

Euromedia

65, Strada Dionisie Lupu
70184 Bucuresti
Tel./Fax 0 12 96 46

BĂLGARIJA

Europress Klassica BK Ltd

66, bd Vitosha
1463 Sofia
Tel./Fax 2 52 74 75

RUSSIA

CCEC

9,60-letiya Oktyabrya Avenue
117312 Moscow
Tel./Fax (095) 135 52 27

CYPRUS

**Cyprus Chamber of Commerce and
Industry**

Chamber Building
38 Grivas Dhigenis Ave
3 Deligiorgis Street
PO Box 1455
Nicosia
Tel. (2) 449500/462312
Fax (2) 458630

MALTA

Miller distributors Ltd

Scots House, M.A. Vassalli street
PO Box 272
Valletta
Tel. 24 73 01
Fax 23 49 14

TÜRKIYE

**Pres Gazete Kitap Dergi
Pazarlama Dağitim Ticaret ve sanayi
AŞ**

Narlibahçe Sokak N. 15
Istanbul-Cağaloğlu
Tel. (1) 520 92 96 - 528 55 66
Fax 520 64 57
Telex 23822 DSVO-TR

ISRAEL

ROY International

PO Box 13056
41 Mishmar Hayarden Street
Tel. Aviv 61130
Tel. 3 496 108
Fax 3 544 60 39

UNITED STATES OF AMERICA/
CANADA

UNIPUB

4611-F Assembly Drive
Lanham, MD 20706-4391
Tel. Toll Free (800) 274 4888
Fax (301) 459 0056

CANADA

Subscriptions only
Uniquement abonnements

Renouf Publishing Co. Ltd

1294 Algoma Road
Ottawa, Ontario K1B 3W8
Tel. (613) 741 43 33
Fax (613) 741 54 39
Telex 0534783

AUSTRALIA

Hunter Publications

58A Gipps Street
Collingwood
Victoria 3066
Tel. (3) 417 5361
Fax (3) 419 7154

JAPAN

Kinokuniya Company Ltd

17-7 Shinjuku 3- Chome
Shinjuku-ku
Tokyo 160-91
Tel. (03) 3439-0121

Journal Department

PO Box 55 Chitose
Tokyo 156
Tel. (03) 3439-0124

SOUTH-EAST ASIA

Legal Library Services Ltd

STK Agency
Robinson Road
PO Box 1817
Singapore 9036

SOUTH AFRICA

Safto

5th Floor, Export House
Cnr Maude & West Streets
Sandton 2146
Tel. (011) 883-3737
Fax (011) 883-6569

AUTRE PAYS
OTHER COUNTRIES
ANDERE LÄNDER

**Office des publications officielles
des Communautés européennes**

2, rue Mercier
L-2985 Luxembourg
Tél. 499 28 -1
Télex PUBOF LU 1324 b
Fax 48 85 73/48 68 17

7/93